D1435776

CRITICAL ENCOUNTERS

CRITICAL ENCOUNTERS

Capitalism, Democracy, Ideas

Wolfgang Streeck

VERSO
London • New York

First published by Verso 2020
© Wolfgang Streeck 2020

1 3 5 7 9 10 8 6 4 2

Earlier versions of the following chapters were published as follows:
1. 'Through Unending Halls', *London Review of Books*, 7 February 2019; 2. 'The Fourth Power', *New Left Review*, no. 110, March/April 2018; 3. *Constellations*, vol. 23, no. 4, 2016; 4. *ILR Review*, vol. 71, no. 2, 2018; 5. 'Playing Catch Up', *London Review of Books*, 4 May 2017; 6. 'Greek to a Greek', *Inference*, vol. 4, no. 3, 2019; 7. 'The Politics of Exit', *New Left Review*, no. 88, July/August 2014; 8. 'Governance heißt das Zauberwort, das alle Konfusion beenden soll', *Frankfurter Allgemeine Zeitung*, 31 March 2015; 9. 'Sonderweg aus der Solidarität', *Süddeutsche Zeitung*, 27 March 2017; 10. 'Scenario for a Wonderful Tomorrow', *London Review of Books*, 30 March 2016; 11. 'Fighting the State', *Development and Change*, vol. 50, no. 3, 2019; 12. 'Sparen um jeden Preis', *Süddeutsche Zeitung*, 24 February 2015; 13. 'You Need a Gun', *London Review of Books*, 14 December 2017; 14. 'What about Capitalism? Jürgen Habermas's Project of a European Democracy', *European Political Science*, vol. 16, no. 2, 2017; 15. 'From Speciation to Specialization', *Social Research*, vol. 85, no. 3, 2018; Chapters 8, 9 and 12 were translated from the German by Rodney Livingstone.

Verso
UK: 6 Meard Street, London W1F 0EG
US: 20 Jay Street, Suite 1010, Brooklyn, NY 11201
versobooks.com

Verso is the imprint of New Left Books

ISBN-13: 978-1-78873-874-3
ISBN-13: 978-1-78873-875-0 (UK EBK)
ISBN-13: 978-1-78873-876-7 (US EBK)

British Library Cataloguing in Publication Data
A catalogue record for this book is available from the British Library

Library of Congress Cataloging-in-Publication Data
A catalog record for this book is available from the Library of Congress

Typeset in Garamond by Biblichor Ltd, Edinburgh
Printed and bound by CPI Group (UK) Ltd, Croydon CR0 4YY

Contents

Books under Review, by Chapter

Preface

CRITICAL ENCOUNTERS is a collection of essays on political economy, stimulated by reading books for review. It is also a celebration of the book as a medium of communication among scholars and with a wider public. Book reviews are occasional productions, not outflows of a specific research project. Someone assumes that somebody else might have something to say about a book deemed important enough to merit extended comment, and if author, title, blurb raise sufficient curiosity, a deal is done. Different book reviews by the same author, as collected in this volume, are therefore only loosely connected: by accident of personal acquaintance, of time believed to be free, or of the reviewer's sense of adventure.

How to review a book that is worthy of being reviewed? For me it requires deep reading, beginning usually with the last chapter, then the introduction, then several expeditions into the interior. This takes time. During reading sessions, I highlight what I find remarkable and sketch my own emerging views in the margins, or on the last pages where the publisher advertises other, often related, books. When I am finished with a book, it looks a little deranged. Having let it sit for a while in this condition, I return to it and read my notes. Where they yield a pattern, for example by repeating themselves, is where the reading has left an impact. Then I begin writing.

Writing book reviews means taking the book seriously as a vehicle of scholarly communication; or, as in my case, even extolling it. In the social sciences, journal articles have come to predominate, which I find deplorable. One hears of university departments that consider candidates with books on their publications list ineligible for appointment – and not only in economics, where writing books brands you as a borderline sociologist (which for a proper economist is the very worst thing that you can be). In my view, article writing is easy compared to book writing. For publication in the form of articles, insights from research may be and frequently are broken down to their smallest publishable units (SPUs), with one-and-a-half pages of 'theory' at the beginning and an even shorter 'discussion' at the end if at all, and in between something on 'method', 'data' and 'results'. Books, by comparison, are drawn-out *Gedankenspiele* – arrangements of long chains of ideas, evolving step by step out of each other. Or a book may develop one dominant idea and access, present and discuss it from ever-new perspectives; reconstruct at length historical sequences and turn them into extensive narratives; offer a wealth of evidence in bright colours – appealing in all of this to the curiosity of readers, their delight in well-told stories and striking, memorable examples. A good book is like a broad canvas, a large tapestry, something to feast on rather than gulp down like a piece of fast food.

Of course, those who care to read a book review want to learn what the book is about and where it belongs in the literature, and their expectations should be honoured. But a worthwhile review of a worthwhile book should also explore what a reader can do with it over and above digesting the facts it reports and the ideas it suggests – where readers-as-users might discover new problems or gain new insights into older ones. As I wrote more and more book reviews, over the years, sometimes transgressing the limits of my own specialist expertise, I began to appreciate the genre for the opportunity it afforded for far-flung, or even speculative, thinking. The necessarily limited length of a book review could provide a good excuse for remaining, in places, suggestive or aphoristic, or for asking questions that one didn't, or couldn't, answer.

By far the majority of the reviews in this collection are 'positive' reviews, meaning that they express respect for the book reviewed and the achievements of its author. I have written 'negative' reviews about books that I thought deserved it; a few examples are included in this volume. But slating a book leaves one with melancholic feelings and should, if only for that reason, be avoided unless necessary: in particular in order to warn potential readers not to believe what isn't worth believing, and authors of further books not to take book-writing too easily. Of course, a book can be wrong in a productive way, or appear to be so to a reviewer, in that readers can learn from considering the book's flaws, how the problems it raises might have been more convincingly solved; but then, a book that lends itself to this cannot really be bad. In any case, having written a few books myself, I never read one expecting perfection. There is always something missing, and even the most outstanding intellectual productions are, *sub specie aeternitatis*, intermediate reports from the frontiers of knowledge preparing the ground, if all goes well, for their future revision. More important and productive than pointing out the weaknesses of a book is to identify its strengths: what one could and should take away from reading it, or in any case what one can use it for if working on or thinking about similar subjects.

Given how much time it takes to complete a book review that does justice to a worthwhile scholarly book, one has to be selective, even if one likes reading books and writing about them. My main criterion is whether I can hope to learn something, either something that further clarifies views I already hold, or something that contradicts those views, planting productive doubts into my subconscious. As one cannot know what exactly is in a book before having read it, selection must rely to an important extent on intuition. A nudge from the outside may be helpful. My favourite example here is my review of Darwin's *Origin of Species*, included in this book as its last chapter and conspicuous at first as strangely unrelated to the others. In fact, I would never have considered engaging with a classic of this intimidating stature had it not been for a journal, *Social Research*, planning a special issue, for which practitioners of the social sciences were asked to write about a book, any book, that they considered significant for their thinking. Working on institutional change I had time and again made contact with theories of evolution but had never really engaged with them in depth. Generally I despised and still despise biologistic accounts of human behaviour, individual and collective, including Spencer's translation of the 'survival of the fittest' principle into a normative prescription for the government of human affairs. On the other hand, I always found evolutionary theory in principle intriguing as a theory of history – natural history – that undertakes to explain change without presuming to predict it, allowing for enough randomness, or indeterminacy, in historical processes to avoid falling into the trap of historical determinism. Hoping to find out more about the exact nature of that theory, and whether a revitalized materialistic macrosociology (which I think is what we urgently need) can learn from it, I proposed that I do *Origin*, and the editors agreed.

Good for me that they did. Working myself into the book, and enjoying the clarity of the writing and the integrity of the exposition of argument and counterargument, it struck me that the theory of 'speciation' as developed by Darwin could be productively compared to the theory of 'specialization' that in one way or other occupies a central position in the classical grand theories of modern society, including those of Smith, Marx, Durkheim,

Spencer and Weber.* Comparing the two, having found hints on how this might be done in Durkheim's *The Division of Labour in Society*, I felt assured that their similarities were far from trivial, indeed extremely revealing, while their differences were equally significant. Taken together, the two suggest the possibility of a humanistic rather than biologistic theory of historical change and societal development, one that is still materialistic while focusing on human society as it evolved out of natural history, a theory that incorporates agency – 'practice' – into its driving forces without falling into the trap of idealistic voluntarism. Allowing for a future with an open horizon, it offers a perspective in which the escape of the human species from biological speciation into social special-ization can be conceived as an accelerating increase of a particularly human adaptive capacity – a perspective that may hold great potential for the long overdue rejuvenation of macrosociology.

While Darwin was special, it seems generally true that taking time to read a well-written book and write about it can teach you something that remains in your memory and shapes your subse-quent thinking in one way or another. The German word for this is *Bildungserlebnis*, weakly translated into English as *educational experience*: an experience that changes the way you see the world, or at least part of it. In no particular order, and picking my exam-ples without seeking to be exhaustive, Bruno Amable's book on France struck me as a wonderful opportunity not just to learn about a country that is not easily accessible to people who do not speak the language. In addition, the book is full of generalizable insights on the state and politics under capitalism, grounded in a narrative of dramatic historical change written to extract from it continuities not just in the historical trajectory of French politics and society but in capitalist political economy generally. Joshua

---

* That there might be a parallel here would have been more difficult to observe working in German, where *Spezialisierung* exists for *specialization* but *speciation* is referred to as *Artenbildung*.

Freeman's history of the factory, for its part, enabled me to see my own experience as a student of industrial sociology and industrial relations in a historical and geographical context; it also added colour to my mental image of the global context of 'Western' industrial development, and it opened up a perspective beyond the world of industrial societies onto that of post-industrial societies. Peter Mair's masterful book on the decay of democratic party politics and party organization in the era of ascending neoliberal globalism, written shortly before his all-too-early death, remains an example for me of how outstanding social science can predict without making predictions: by analysing a historical configuration and the forces at work in it so well that what would later emerge out of it – here: the rise of 'populism' in 'Western' democratic politics – can be recognized as the natural consequence, even though it was not yet in evidence when the book was written.

Equally impressive was Quinn Slobodian's book on the 'globalists', which synthesizes and organizes into a broad historical picture what many of us knew only in a much more fragmented way about neoliberalism as a social and political movement dating from the first half of the twentieth century. Indefatigably fighting the nation-state as a potential stronghold of democratic socialism, with the inevitable distortions it was prone to inflict on free markets, in the 1990s it finally prevailed, at least temporarily, over its last remaining opponents. Of particular interest to me was what I found there about the European Union and its ambivalent status in neoliberal politics as a regional experiment in anti-nationalism and anti-statism on the one hand and a potential breeding ground of supranationalism and multinational state-formation on the other – an ambivalence that was settled with the neoliberal turn of the EU in the 1990s. Having read the book, I was able to see the extensive specialist literature on 'European integration', to which I had earlier contributed, with different eyes – wondering how professional social scientists can be as forgetful as they sometimes are about the politics of what they so painstakingly analyse and 'theorize'. Similarly eye-opening, if in a different way, I found reviewing Jürgen Habermas's essay on 'technocracy'. In grappling with it I realized more clearly than ever before how thin democracy becomes, as a concept, if taken out of its historical context – here that of globalized capitalism – and in particular if the capitalist economy is conceived as an economic system governed by economic laws, rather than as a transgressive social structure of power and privilege from which society and social life need to be protected.

What I agree is controversial – and I have more than once been guilty of it – is using, or perhaps abusing, a book review as an opportunity to say something that one believes needs to be said although its connection to the book being reviewed is no more than tenuous. My article on Martin Sandbu's fine book on 'the future of the euro and the politics of debt' in Europe can probably serve as a case in point. That the largest part of my review essay is about the immigration policy of the Merkel government may be justified, and is so justified in the text, as illustrating how, if push comes to shove, the domestic politics of Germany as the hegemonic member state of the European Union, driven by national political needs and interests, may hit the other member states unprepared and wreak havoc on the Union as a whole. As Sandbu's main point is that the euro could be rescued by member states emancipating themselves from the EU centre – meaning Germany – and acting more independently on their own, I wanted to demonstrate by recounting the 2015 open borders episode how unlikely it was that this would ever be possible under the existing European Union regime.[*]

---

[*] A similar intention is behind my review, written in part tongue-in-cheek, of the book by Johannes Becker and Clemens Fuest which culminates in 'a pragmatic proposal to solve the euro crisis'. To me the book represents a distinct category of work on the euro by mainstream German economists – a category in which it stands out for its theoretical precision and empirical perceptiveness. While its authors are fully aware of

Another explanation, and perhaps apology, may be due for my discussion of the books on the German economy by Werner Plumpe, David Audretsch and Erik Lehmann, and Franz-Josef Meiers. Apart from the fact that I wholeheartedly disagree with some of the authors' main points, I thought it necessary to suggest a very different approach to German economic exceptionalism: one that takes into account not just the longer-term history of Germany as a late industrializer and an over-industrialized national economy, but also as a thoroughly defeated would-be empire after 1945. The advantage I see in my approach is that it avoids blaming the sometimes admittedly strange – from an Anglo-American viewpoint – obsessions of German economic policy with avoiding debt and balancing budgets in the manner of the 'Swabian house-wife' on a nationally specific lack of economic savvy and a deplorable inability to get one's own interests right. (It also renders unnecessary accounting for the superior performance of German industry under the euro by 'nationalist' German industrial unions sacrificing the interests of their members to the national goal of a high export surplus.) To make this point, I felt I needed to venture

---

the deep institutional flaws of the euro under the Maastricht Treaty, they stop short of saying that its crisis cannot be solved as long as the euro remains a single currency for differently organized national economies politically governed by still sovereign nation-states. Rather than drawing the lessons of their analysis, however, they limit themselves to proposing 'reforms' which, as things stand, and as they must know, will never become reality. In part this may be due to a politically naïve optimism inherent in an economics-trained worldview, with its underlying assumption that what is 'rational' (as identified unambiguously by economic 'science') must also be possible. On a less heroic note, it may reflect a quite realistic fear of being identified and outcast by colleagues, politics, the press and relevant funding agencies as 'anti-European', in a country whose prosperity has increasingly come to depend on the common European currency. Being seen as 'anti-European' in Germany brings with it unpleasant consequences – so much so that when it comes to 'solving the euro crisis', advisors asked for advice may find it advisable to suggest the impossible and leave it to the politicians to discover that it cannot be done; which has the additional advantage that the refusal of the crisis to go away can be blamed by economic science on economically incompetent or electorally opportunistic politics.

into a longish exposition especially on the relationship between social structures and economic 'competitiveness', emphasizing the dramatic 'modernization' of the (West) German way of life as a result of the defeat, the occupation, and in particular the demographic revolution in the Western part of the country caused by the expulsion of millions of Germans from what then became parts of the Soviet Union, Poland and Czechoslovakia.

I leave it to readers to decide whether and to what extent the fifteen reviews collected in this book are more than accidentally related to each other and what general themes, if any, keep the volume together. That different people might find different commonalities or, as the case may be, incompatibilities does not necessarily pose a problem for someone like me who habitually hesitates to sacrifice empirical variety for theoretical unity, preferring not to lose contact with the multiple facets of an ontologically incoherent social reality. The grouping of the book's fifteen essays in three categories, 'Capitalism', 'Democracy' and 'Ideas', is not entirely systematic and nothing particular should be read into it. Other arrangements are equally conceivable but would be equally arbitrary. Whatever thematic clusters might be identified, they would always overlap. There is, for example, a sustained interest across the chapters in the political economy and the ideational foundations of neoliberalism; in the functioning of the European Union, in particular the European Monetary Union, and its effects on European societies, their states and the relations between them; in the impact of a capitalist economy on democratic politics and vice versa; and, not to forget, in the peculiar characteristics and idiosyncrasies of the German economy and the resulting politics of Germany in Europe and the European Union.

Appended to the book are six of the monthly *Letters from Europe* I have written for the online Spanish journal *El Salto*. The letters comment on current events around the European Union, small and large. Included are those from December 2019 to May 2020, the reason being that quite a few of the chapters in this book deal with the politics of 'Europe', which are changing at a tremendous rate. Until the book world has caught up with the EU's extraordinary and deepening crisis, one is left with such commentary-on-the-move. Nothing about the EU response to the pandemic will come as a surprise to readers of my scholarly work and political comment on the 'European project'. The way it came about, however, is extraordinary and deserves to be recalled so that we can measure the follies of the past against what happened later.

All things considered, then, *Critical Encounters* is a somewhat mixed bag and certainly not a 'theory' of anything. No need to read it in one piece, from cover to cover. But these sporadic explorations of not yet systematically related subjects may perhaps prepare the ground for something more ambitious in the future.

PART I

Capitalism

. . . the More They Stay the Same

February 2019

IT WAS IN THE early 1960s, I think, that our class at a small-town gymnasium made a trip to southwestern Germany, herded by several of our teachers. We visited Heidelberg and Schwetzingen and similar places, without really seeing them; seventeen-year-old boys have other things to consider. However, we also went to Rüsselsheim, near Frankfurt, for a tour of the Opel car factory. Never in my wildest dreams had I imagined a place like this: the deafening noise, the dirt, the heat, and in the middle of it all, living people stoically performing predefined minute operations on the cars-in-the-making that were slowly but relentlessly moving by their workstations. The high point of the visit was the foundry, located in the basement – which, as I now learn from Joshua Freeman's marvelous book, was the way car factories were then designed.* Here, where the heat seemed unbearable and there was almost no light, half-naked human beings carried, in small buckets of obviously back-breaking weight, the molten metal, red-hot, from the furnace to the casting stations. To me, trained in

---

* Joshua Freeman, *Behemoth: A History of the Factory and the Making of the Modern World*, New York and London: W. W. Norton, 2018.

the classics rather than the real world, it seemed as if I had entered the workshop of Hephaistos, Homer's crippled Olympian black-smith. Looking back, I think it was on that day that I began to become something like a radical and decided to study sociology, which I then believed could enable me and others to help improve the lives of those having to slave away in the basements of the factories of this world.

Later, as a young social scientist, the car industry remained an obsession for me. I included car manufacturing in my empirical work whenever I could, and made a point of visiting the factories to renew my 'feel' for them and replenish my supply of mental images of what I tried, often in vain, to convince my colleagues were the Gothic cathedrals of the twentieth century. What I found amazing, among other things, was how these places were changing, and how fast, compared to what I had seen back in the 1960s: less and less noise, dirt and dust; much better air; no welding by hand and no overhead assembly anymore; hermetically sealed automatic paint shops; the heavy lifting all done by machines and later by robotics. In final assembly it was now the workers who were lifted up, sitting on movable platforms along with the doors or seats or whatever else they were installing. My last visit to the VW plant at Wolfsburg, more than three decades ago, ended as usual in final assembly, where no sound was to be heard apart from soft music and the first firing of the engines at the end of the line as the new cars were taken away to the storage area. The workers were mostly women, dressed in jeans and t-shirts. With a big smile and the male chauvinism that will always be part of the culture of car making, my guide, from the all-powerful works council, let me know that what I was seeing was 'Wolfsburg's marriage market': 'The lads drop by here when they have a break to see what's on offer'.

Of course, much of this change was due to technological progress, and also to labour market constraints like the need to feminize the workforce and the labour process. But politics and industrial relations were at least as important. In the 1970s, after the strike wave of 1968 and 1969, governments, managements and trade unions in European manufacturing countries began to take seriously demands for what in Germany came to be called *Humanisierung der Arbeit* – the 'humanization' of industrial work. Under Brandt and Schmidt, this became a national research and development campaign, run out of a special department in the Ministry of Research and Technology, which lavishly funded academic and industrial projects in engineering, management and industrial sociology. Ending Taylorism was the object, and there were results, especially where workers and their representatives had rights, not just to information and consultation, but also to co-decision-making on work organization, technology, working time, training and the like.

Freeman, whose history centres on the UK, the US, the USSR and China, largely sidesteps the European continent, which is regrettable given the enduring success of manufacturing in countries like Germany and Sweden. Certainly workforce participation and anti-Taylorism had their drawbacks, as did worker co-management. In Sweden, work reform culminated in avantgarde production methods at Volvo and Saab that were not only expensive but were disliked by the workers they were supposed to benefit – like 'group work' on 'production islands', where complete cars were individually put together almost from scratch and workers were encouraged to sign 'their' product with their names. For a while, Saabs and Volvos were the favourite cars of European intellectuals because they were made, it was believed, by 'happy workers' – until both firms returned to more conventional work organization (which, however, did not in the end protect them from being taken over by GM and Ford, respectively). In Germany, meanwhile, cooperation between management and the works council at Volkswagen gradually deteriorated into collusion and co-optation. The scandals included multimillion euro payments to the head of the works council and his girlfriend, authorized by the company's personnel director, Peter Hartz. (In 2002, while at VW,

Hartz was appointed by Gerhard Schröder to chair a commission on the labour market, which eventually led to the 'Hartz-IV' reforms, which cut benefits for the long-term unemployed.) Still, on the shop floor this mattered less than in the press, and whatever else it was that management, union and works council did together, the workers who no longer had to work overhead surely appreciated that.

Freeman's book tells a long and elaborate story that begins in England in the late eighteenth century, then moves to the United States, and from textiles to steel and from there to automobiles, and on to the worldwide victory of Taylorism and Fordism in the first half of the twentieth century. That victory extended even into the Soviet Union under Stalin, and peaked in the mass production of the Second World War. This, in turn, was followed by the Cold War and the hopes that accompanied it for peaceful global convergence driven by the inherent constraints and opportunities of modern industrialism, until history moved on with the rise of China and its peculiar pathway of industrial modernity. Throughout his account, Freeman manages to convey the deep ambivalence associated with modernization as industrialization: expulsion from the land, proletarianization, exploitation, repression, cruel discipline on the one hand and emancipation from traditional ways of life on the other, coming with money wages, new solidarities, trade unions fighting for higher wages and better conditions, and with the possibility of industrial citizenship and social rights gained by supporting and participating in popular politics of social reform.

Among the things that make Freeman's book special is that he pays attention, not just to the internal organization of factories, but also to their relationship with, and indeed their effect on, their surrounding societies. That factories require particular patterns of settlement – large new cities or extensive company housing – does not always figure prominently in accounts of industrialization. Planning for the sudden arrival of large numbers of people in a previously sparsely populated geographical space attracted urbanists with progressive visions of a new society and a new industrial man or woman requiring, and thriving from, access to collective infrastructures, entertainment, education and culture: a modern lifestyle in sharp contrast to the villages where the first generation of industrial workers, mostly young, were recruited. Architects could design factory buildings not just to meet utilitarian requirements but to make aesthetic statements about the value of what was produced inside them. Factory architecture, we learn from Freeman, especially as it developed in the United States, soon became an international style that eventually spread even to the Soviet Union, where factories were designed to represent and celebrate the same industrial modernity that was taking shape under Western capitalism.

Freeman's account of 'the making of the modern world' opens our eyes to the enormous extent of international cross-fertilization, especially in the 1930s and 1940s, not just between the United States and the USSR, when large-scale manufacturing was developing into a world of its own, with Henry Ford as a global icon of universal progress. One of his admirers was, of course, Adolf Hitler. Immediately upon taking power Hitler had tried hard but in vain to make German auto manufacturers abandon their traditional style of small-scale craft production and produce a simple car 'for the people', a *Volkswagen*. In the end it had to be Ford himself who helped him set up the first Fordist German car plant (apart from the two much smaller Ford and General Motors plants in Cologne and Rüsselsheim), at a place later named Wolfsburg, with second-hand machinery from Dearborn, Michigan. To show his gratitude, in 1938 Hitler awarded Ford the highest decoration of the Nazi regime for foreigners, the Great Cross of the German Order of the Eagle *(Großkreuz des Deutschen Adlerordens)*.

Another feature of Freeman's story, also unusual, is the space he devotes to the representation of the factory in the arts, beginning with the futurism of the interwar years. Particularly prominent were photography and cinematography, the most modern branches

of artistic production, whose works were as technologically repro-
ducible as the new mass consumer products. While photographers
and film-makers did document the drudgery of mass production
and the misery of exploitation, they were no less fascinated by the
promise of progress embodied in the newly minted cars coming
off the conveyor belt, the polished airplane engines and turbines
ready to start, and the huge workshops with their avant-garde
architecture, like Frank Lloyd Wright's Johnson Wax Factory in
Racine, Wisconsin, where hundreds of people could be seen to be
working together in quiet discipline for American and universal
improvement.

One question that reappears at each turning point of Freeman's
long story is whether the suffering in the factories of early industrialization was really necessary for, and must therefore be justified
by, the progress of industrialism and, with it, of mankind. This
debate begins with none less than Adam Smith, who discusses the
pros and cons of the division of labour, the increase in productivity and the decline in humanity it simultaneously portends – so
that at some point the progress of the former is undone by the
damage done to the latter, by chopping away at human mental
capacities and personal self-esteem. In the West, it was capitalists
who insisted that the waste of one or two generations in the living
hell of the factories of Manchester and then the world was a sacrifice that had to be made for a better life for all in the future. But
where can that sacrifice end if the systemic imperative of capitalism is the endless accumulation of capital? This was not necessarily
an issue under socialism: both Stalin and Trotsky considered the
use of brutal force indispensable for a socialist variant of primitive
accumulation, meaning unfettered reliance on Taylorism and
military-style discipline to advance the formation of a socialist
working class. The promise was that with the arrival of
Communism, the toil would be over, as society would be liberated
from work by a combination of socialized fixed capital and Soviet
power. European social democrats, for their part, settled for

liberation mainly *in* rather than *from* work, with less managerial discretion, shorter chains of command, job enlargement, group work, use of productivity gains to slow down the work pace, and the like. The results were observed by a new generation of industrial sociologists, in the wake of the worker uprisings of the 1960s and 1970s.

Not surprisingly, a prominent theme in Freeman's account is the conflict between labour and capital, or management, over factory organization and factory discipline, and above all over how to share the proceeds from the superior productivity of organized cooperation in large-scale production. Factory work is teamwork, making it impossible to devise a simple formula for dividing its benefits, and opening the door for bargaining between parties with conflicting demands and interests. Here a crucial parameter is relative power, as brought to bear in, as well as affected by, national and local institutions of industrial relations. A pervasive force in factory life, power extends to and shapes the organization of production even where one would not necessarily expect it. Freeman recounts how in the post-war era giant factories began to go out of fashion in the United States, to be replaced by much smaller, geographically dispersed production sites. Changed transportation and coordination technologies helped make this possible, as did vertical disintegration and just-in-time delivery of ever more parts contracted out to a growing supply industry. But these were only facilitating circumstances; the driving force, according to Freeman, was the response of managements to the power organized labour had been allowed to build under the New Deal, most effectively where factories were large. To avoid costly concessions to their newly empowered workforces, firms shifted to greenfield sites in places where the labour supply was not yet spoiled by a tradition of unionization. Here, 'human resource management' could choose from 100,000 job applications for an initial workforce of 1,500, making sure that those finally hired were anti-union, had a family with children, and had to pay off a mortgage for their family home – on the plausible assumption that a mortgage makes for a robust work ethic and at a minimum militates against going on strike.

More as an aside, Freeman notes that management flight from large factories was not universal. It didn't happen in countries and companies with effective institutions of industrial democracy, where worker representatives could veto job relocation while at the same time guaranteeing management industrial peace, and indeed collaboration, in return. Here a prime example is, again, Volkswagen's main factory at Wolfsburg, which did not just remain big but in recent years has actually expanded its workforce, from 44,000 in 2007 to 62,000 ten years later (a little less than Freeman claims), at a time when the company was also growing rapidly through internationalization. To a large extent, this was possible because the union was able to extract from management new investment and employment guarantees for the Wolfsburg plant, in exchange for its services as an effective manager of worker discontent. Another factor was that the *Land* of Niedersachsen, where Wolfsburg is located, is a privileged shareholder in Volkswagen and sufficiently powerful in this capacity to ensure that enough of the company's jobs remain where its present workers and their families live and vote. (This is a condition that the European Union has for years tried to put an end to, in the name of 'free movement of capital'.)

Of course, it is not just management that may find factories of that size scary; workers may as well, in particular if they have nothing to say inside them. An interesting experience I recall from the late 1970s was taking a British trade union officer to Wolfsburg for a tour of the factory. Coming from the doomed, geographically dispersed, never really integrated, effectively stand-alone small British Leyland plants of the time, torn by industrial strife and dependent on heavy public subsidies, he grew increasingly depressed as we walked through the seemingly unending factory halls – until he burst out to complain about the inhuman enormity of so many people pressed into one industrial plant. His frustration increased when a question regarding the extent to which the plant reached its production target on an average day went unanswered, since his German counterparts had no concept of production targets ever not being met. In the evening over a beer, he found relief in violating the first commandment of Fawlty Towers and telling us about the war ('Back then when you fellows didn't behave'): as a member of a small special unit of the British Marine Corps, he had landed in Flensburg to arrest Großadmiral Dönitz, an act of heroism for which, to his surprise, we expressed our deeply felt gratitude.

Freeman's final chapter is on the 'giant factories' of Asia, in particular the Taiwanese-owned Foxconn plant, or plants, in Mainland China. Here, too, size is not a problem, made possible, not by industrial democracy, but by industrial repression. As behoves a historian, Freeman places the contemporary labour constitution of China in the context of recent Chinese history, in particular the Cultural Revolution under Mao Zedong, when management was to be subordinated to the will of the masses and factory discipline replaced with revolutionary ardour. Nothing of that is left today, except for the fact that the harsh regime in the fast-growing private sector of Chinese manufacturing may be explained, in part, as an outgrowth of the economic and political disasters of the 1960s and 1970s.

Looking at Europe in particular, there seems to be yet another, even more sinister connection between the politics of liberation in its Western version (if not *from* then *in* work) and the new 'Asian mode of production'. As satisfied consumers of the electronic toys, colourful running shoes and cheap t-shirts that come to us courtesy of modern Asian industrialism, we tend to forget about how they are produced in Shenzhen, Chengdu, Zhengzhou, in Saigon in Vietnam, and in Taiwan, Indonesia, Cambodia and Myanmar – in factories not owned but directed by firms like Apple, Disney, Adidas and Walmart. Manchester still exists, but on the global periphery, too far away for school excursions. It is to there that we have externalized the misery of long hours and low wages, enabling us as consumers to reap their benefits without bearing the costs as producers, and disregarding for the moment those that, in an ironic version of liberation *from* work, lost their jobs in the process.

Much of what Freeman writes in this impressively well-written chapter may already have been familiar from occasional reports in the media. But seeing it presented together in one piece makes for a truly upsetting experience. Plants with between 300,000 and 400,000 workers; a factory with a workforce of 350,000 producing iPhones and nothing else; a regime of residence permits for migrant workers designed to prevent them from organizing; the dormitories with their strict, nineteenth-century-American style of quasi-military discipline. No cities of the future here: only barbed wire, uniformed security guards and surveillance cameras. And the suicides of which some of us may have read: when, for example, in 2010, thirteen young workers jumped to their death from the roof of a Foxconn factory producing iPhones and iPads. Freeman reports how Apple politely pointed its finger at Foxconn, and how Foxconn responded with preventive measures to spare its biggest customer further embarrassment, installing mesh wire on the roofs and balconies of its factory buildings and putting up 3 million square metres of netting above the ground all around them to catch and thereby save anyone desperate enough to find a way, still, to try to kill themselves.

One interesting question that Freeman discusses is why those Asian factories are so big, making it necessary for their rulers to expend so much effort on controlling the workers. According to Freeman, this is not due to economies of scale; production processes are not complex enough to justify organizations of that size. More likely it is the nature of the outsourcing relationship dominated by customers like Nike and Hewlett-Packard and the way these companies work their markets, where 'flexibility' is everything. When Apple made its long-awaited iPhone 6 available to its eager devotees, it had to be able to sell 13 million units in its first three days on the market. Since 'freshness', according to Apple's Tim Cook, is a modern gadget's most important property, final changes in design must be possible until a few weeks before sales begin. Just-in-time production of this sort needs huge factories with huge workforces kept, as it were, in storage, in company-owned dormitories nearby, to be called out any time and ordered on short notice to work, if required, twelve-hour shifts or longer for several consecutive weeks. Nowhere is the secret of how we can pay for what we are made to believe we need, while being spared the pain of producing it at prices we can afford, laid bare more clearly than it is here.

Not that Freeman leaves his readers without hope. While wages have recently increased, labour turnover continues to be extremely high, indicating a degree of worker dissatisfaction that may become too costly for employers to sustain. The number and size of strikes at Chinese factories seems considerable, giving the lie to the idea of the submissive Chinese worker. Freeman argues that a 'civilizing effect' has always been associated with factory life. By moving away from the village and earning their own money, even in the most dismal of circumstances, the sons and daughters of peasants escape what Marx and Engels called 'the idiocy of rural life'. Could modernization, its manifold discontents notwithstanding, spread from the factory to society in China, as it may have done before in other places?

Historians deal with the past; the future is not their turf. Still, at the end of Freeman's outstanding book readers might have expected a few reflections, or speculations, on what may be next in the long story of organized work and production. Clearly the 'satanic mills' of Foxconn – set up at the behest of, among others, Apple, the greatest capitalist firm of all time – are one part of the picture, and undoubtedly a major one. Equally interesting, however, is an entirely new kind of factory, or quasi-factory, where the bulk of the productive capital is no longer centrally owned and factory discipline is replaced with the discipline of the market. In the world of the new platform firm, of the Uber and TaskRabbit kind, it is not a master capitalist who owns the means of production but rather (I am tempted to say, once again) the skilled worker on the frontline – at least by the time she has paid off the loan awarded to her by the firm to invest in her contribution to its physical equipment. Production is local, close to the customer, indeed customized. There is no agglomeration any more, not of production, or of workers and their living spaces. Only management is centralized at the global level. But like the utopian projects of the 1970s that were intended to restore the dignity of the factory worker, management now issues advice, not orders: it helps workers get their jobs done and services workers instead of pushing them around. Workers, in turn, work when they want, and the 'alienation' of their work from their lives, so characteristic of the factory of the industrial age, is forever a thing of the past.

Or so it appears, or is made to appear. On second thought, the Taylorist separation of planning and execution, as so brilliantly analysed by someone like Harry Braverman, may nowhere be more rigid than in the new platform firms, where the tools of planning are solely and incontestably in the hands of management, incorporated as a separate firm. Execution, meanwhile, planned and coordinated by that firm, is left to subcontractors controlled, not just by material incentives, but by the latest behavioural technologies embodied in proprietary algorithms stored in the latest, also proprietary, remote-control equipment. Rather than social life reintegrating work, the now virtual factory integrates workers' private spaces into the sphere of production. In extreme cases, life can be turned into work without those working-by-living becoming aware of it. One example is the 'users' of Facebook, its customers, who inadvertently produce Facebook's most important resource, the data left as indelible traces of their increasingly virtual lifeways. Another is the hundreds of thousands of would-be 'influencers' who spend their days producing pictures and videos endorsing industrial products, in the hope of eventually being paid for it by their producers.

Traditional categories, such as wage labour or the labour market, easily reach their limits here and are at risk of becoming meaningless. In the giant decentralized service factory, you are given a socially networked opportunity to do work – this work can include what we produce for Apple, Google, Facebook, Tinder and the like, believing that we are 'using' them when actually we are being used ourselves. Is there in this world a role for labour law, for social protection, collective protest and power, voice before exit – in other words, politics? Can we hope for the return of the independent craftsperson of yesteryear, ready to organize in modern guilds and resurrected trade unions, or of the gang system of the docks or the aircraft industry as it still existed half a century ago in Britain and, to a lesser extent, the United States? Or can, perhaps, civil law take the place of labour law in regulating the new factories? If our societies still see it as their task to civilize the world of organized production, they had better get working on it, now.

CHAPTER 2

The Fourth Power?

March 2018

LIKE BLOOD IN GOETHE'S *FAUST*, money 'is a very special fluid'. It circulates in the body political-economic, whose sustenance depends on its liquidity. And it is surrounded by mystery. In fact, money is easily the most unpredictable and least governable human institution we have ever known. Allegedly invented as a general equivalent, to serve as an accounting unit, means of exchange and store of value, it has over time penetrated into the remotest corners of social life, constantly assuming new forms and springing fresh surprises. Even Keynes had to admit that his attempt at *A Treatise on Money* (1930) ran into 'many problems and perplexities'. How money came to be what it is today, in capitalist modernity, may perhaps with the benefit of hindsight be reconstructed as a process of progressive dematerialization and abstraction, accompanied by growing commodification and state sponsorship. But how money *functions* in its present historical form is more difficult to say; where it is going from here, harder still. This social construction has always been beset with, and driven by, unanticipated consequences – caused by human action, but not controlled by it.

Money, the product of finance, is an enigma and always has been. Even the chief engineers of the revitalization of global capitalism by way of its financialization in the late twentieth century, the Alan Greenspans and Gordon Browns, did not know what was growing under their hands. To reassure themselves – and everyone else – they resolved that 'market participants' would, if left to pursue their own interests, build the most stable of all possible financial worlds. Public regulators merely had to clean up the mess whenever a bubble burst, as it inevitably would. Debates about the causes and consequences of the 2008 collapse have so far had little effect on the direction of long-term underlying trends. The global money supply continues to expand considerably faster than the world economy, as it has since the 1970s. Broad money was 59 per cent of global GDP in 1970, 104 per cent in 2000 and 125 per cent in 2015; and yet there has been almost no inflation in the leading capitalist economies since the 1980s, even though interest rates are at record lows – close to zero, sometimes even negative. Nobody can really explain this. Indeed, discussions are still ongoing about what caused the high inflation of the 1920s and – less dramatic – the 1970s. What *is* growing, alongside money, is debt: up from 246 per cent of global GDP in 2000 to 321 per cent in 2016. This includes both public and private debt. Public debt increased markedly after 2008, while private household debt in the United States now exceeds the GDP of China, itself one of the most indebted countries in the world. Debt is a promise of future repayment with interest: a promise that one must believe. While it is clear that there must be a limit to debt – the point at which the promise of repayment becomes unrealistic – nobody knows exactly where this limit is, nor what would happen if it was exceeded.

Joseph Vogl's *The Ascendancy of Finance* does not try to settle these questions.* What it does do, however, is lead us into the

---

* Joseph Vogl, *The Ascendancy of Finance*, trans. Simon Garnett, Cambridge: Polity, 2017

heart of darkness of today's financialized capitalism, the place where money is made and whence it spreads. A professor of German literature at Humboldt University, Berlin, Vogl was a translator of Foucault, Deleuze and Lyotard in the 1990s, and has since focused on the inter-relations of political philosophy, literature and economic theory. *Kalkul und Leidenschaft* (2008) analysed the marriage of Enlightenment-era 'calculus and passion' in *Leviathan*, *Wilhelm Meister* and Lillo's *London Merchant*. Two years later, *Das Gespenst des Kapitals* (published in English as *Spectre of Capital*) detected a strain of secularized theodicy within liberal economic thought which Vogl dubbed *Oikodizee*. Now, in *The Ascendancy of Finance*, Vogl skips over money's long prehistory and social anthropology – on cowry shells and camels, see, *inter alia*, David Graeber, *Debt: The First 5,000 Years* (2011) – to transport the reader to the early modern period, which saw the rise of both the modern state and large-scale finance.

That their births coincided, Vogl argues, is no accident. State power and finance are, in fact, Siamese twins, sometimes at odds with one another but always interdependent. Money is, as it were, the oldest public–private partnership: at one and the same time private property and public good; tradeable commodity and central bank monopoly; credit and debt; a creature of the market and of the 'grey area' between market and state. The relationship undergoes continuous permutation. Yet despite its ever-changing and often downright bizarre forms, money can be traced to just two sources, both located in the force-field between states and markets. One is the creativity of all sorts of traders seeking new devices – to cut transaction costs, in the modern jargon – from promissory notes to bitcoin, assisted and exploited in equal measure by a growing financial sector which buys and sells, for profit, the commercial paper used by traders to extend credit to one another. The second is the need of states to finance their activities through debt or taxes – usually both – and to keep their economies in good health by providing businesses with safe means of exchange and abundant opportunities for what Marx calls 'plus-making'. How these processes work together to create modern money is impressively described by Vogl over two chapters.

Money speaks, it is said, and its first words are always: trust me. Given the obscure circumstances of its production, this seems to be asking a lot. As economic exchange became more extended and opportunities for confidence tricks – from John Law to Standard and Poor's – proliferated, so trust in money, essential for the capitalist economy, had to be safeguarded by state authority. States, or their rulers, have since time immemorial made money trustworthy by certifying it with their stamp of approval. This afforded them an opening to appropriate a fraction of its value in the form of what is called seigniorage, as well as providing manifold occasions for abuse, such as debasing the currency. An important contribution to the credibility of states as stewards of money was the seventeenth-century invention of permanent public debt, in parallel with the transition from personal to parliamentary rule and the introduction of regular taxation. These developments guaranteed the state's creditors the reliable servicing of outstanding balances. Public debt could now be subdivided into low-denomination debt certificates, and these could circulate as means of payment, because the state could be trusted to accept them in payment of taxes, or in exchange for whatever it had promised to deliver when issuing its debt as currency. Moreover, private credit as extended by banks to trustworthy debtors could be denominated in public debt, making the sovereign state the economy's debtor of last resort.

Today's money of paper notes and electronic ledgers represents a complex pyramid of private and public promises of future settlement of present accounts, secured and securitized in virtually unending chains of formal contracts and informal understandings. How could people – and peoples – have entrusted their lives to this dubious co-production of banks and states, this accident-prone social construction, despite the long history of financial scandals and crises extending from the seventeenth century to our own times? In elegant historical-institutionalist fashion, Vogl recounts the long story of modern money's development, tracing the co-evolution of sovereign states and financial markets – each needing the other in defence of its own credit and credibility. Drawing on impressive historical and philosophical erudition, Vogl sets out from early modern theorists of the state and state sovereignty – we encounter *inter alia* Montchrétien, Naudé, Malebranche, Leibniz, Rousseau, Smith. They are read in the light of the heavy dependence of public finance and national economic prosperity on the goodwill of private capitalists – the latter, in turn, reliant on the state's readiness to use its monopoly of legitimate violence in support of enterprising financial adventurers who, like alchemists, transmute the dirt of debt into the gold of legal tender.

A critical manoeuvre in Vogl's conceptual strategy is his radical break with the liberal antinomy of states and markets, or politics and the economy, insisting instead on their historical and systemic interdependence: no state sovereignty without credit; no credible finance without sovereign reinsurance. This is why he pays no attention to utopian projects of reform aimed at terminating money's public–private dualism: either by privatizing it à la Hayek or, as it were, 'statizing' it along the lines proposed by Irving Fisher in *100% Money* (1935) or the current *Vollgeld* (sovereign money) movement. Money lives and grows and becomes profitable by what Vogl – in the title of the German original – calls the *Souveränitätseffekt*, which radiates from the sovereign state onto the wheeling and dealing of the financial marketplace, backing up these contractual transactions with coercive public authority. In this way, Vogl more or less explicitly writes off the good old orthodox Marxist distinction between base and superstructure (indeed, following Foucault, the base – in the sense of the overall organization of production and consumption, is absent from Vogl's picture). Finance can only be what it is if it partakes in the state, and the state develops into a value-creating economic agent as it extracts seigniorage from its money production and invites the financial industry to cash in. In fact, according to Vogl, states became sovereign by co-opting finance into their emerging sovereignty and parcelling out part of that sovereignty to the markets, thereby creating a private enclave within public authority endowed with a sovereignty of its own. Just as modern society could not have been monetized without state authority, so the state could only become society's executive committee by making finance the executive committee of the state.

Money, then, emerges in what Vogl calls 'zones of indeterminacy', where private and public interests are reconciled by assigning public status to the former and privatizing the latter. The result is a complex interlocking of conflict and cooperation generative of, and benefiting from, what Vogl calls 'seigniorial power' – a relationship in which the state and finance undertake to govern one another and, together, society at large. Zones of indeterminacy, Vogl writes, 'have an ambiguous relation to both sides, they are encouraged and restricted by state authority, they can either boost or inhibit the exercise of political power, and they can stimulate or obstruct (for example through monopolization) market mechanisms'. Financial systems need state regulation to remain responsible and trustworthy, but too much regulation drives money away and thereby undermines the viability of the state. States, in turn, don't just need robust banking systems for the economy but also for credit for themselves, for which they must be in a credible position to promise conscientious repayment, with interest. If they default, they may lose access to financial markets, and their financial industry – and perhaps that of allied countries too – may have to default as well.

It is in crisis situations, when banks are about to collapse or states teeter on the edge of insolvency, that the liberal notion of a clear distinction between markets and the state is exposed as a myth. On such occasions, as financial and political elites join forces in a virtual boardroom, functional differentiation – the pet category of functionalist sociology – loses its meaning and sovereignty reveals a Schmittian face, declaring a state of emergency and *die Stunde der Exekutive*. As Vogl shows in his account of the Wall Street 'rescue operation' of autumn 2008, in the hour of the executive, huge public funds suddenly become available to exclusive circles of bankers and their presumptive overseers. Working together as the clock ticks, they take command decisions whose consequences nobody can predict in an effort to maintain at least the appearance of control over events, and to prevent the pyramid of promises that is financialized capitalism from collapsing under the weight of mounting suspicion that it might have become unmanageable.

In calmer times, the two poles of seigniorial power – the state and the market – meet and merge in the central bank, the hybrid institutional core of capitalism's 'zone of indeterminacy'. Vogl offers concise, but for that reason all the more impressive, comparative histories of the Bank of England, the Federal Reserve, the Bundesbank, the Banco Central de Chile under Pinochet and the European Central Bank. Such bodies mediate between the financial market's need for state backing and the state's reliance on capitalist assistance in the form of a healthy financial industry that can serve as a conduit for the administration of monetary policy and the delivery of capital to all sectors of the economy. Private outposts in the state and public outposts in finance, central banks have historically moved back and forth between very different institutional forms: private, public and various combinations of the two. Far from constituting a rational-functionalist formation, they have performed widely diverse and often barely related functions – from the administration of state debt to the issuing of currency and the supervision of private banks – cobbled together more or less ad hoc according to political expediency, just as one would expect in a world of 'indeterminacy'. What distinguishes them as a type is that they exist to protect finance from the fickleness of political rulers – absolutist or democratic – while providing the latter with at least the illusion of control over the fickleness of financial markets. Institutional independence is crucial, nowadays meaning above all insulation from electoral politics. Monetary questions must be de-politicized – which is to say, de-democratized. Central banks, Vogl argues, constitute a fourth power, overshadowing legislature, executive and judiciary, and integrating financial market mechanisms into the practice of government.

Central banks' claim to autonomous authority is based on their assumed, and asserted, technical competence. As they and their *aficionados* in the media and in economics departments are fond of telling us, central bankers know things about the economy that normal people, inevitably overwhelmed by such complexity, cannot even begin to fathom. They command theories with which to make the economy do what is in society's best interest – in the long run at least, when regrettably we will all be dead. Central bankers themselves have always been aware, although they hide it as best they can from the unwashed, that central banking is 'not a science but an art'. This means that what they sell to the public as a quasi-natural science is in fact nothing more than intuitive empathy, an ability acquired by long having moved in the right circles to sense how capital will feel, good or bad, about what a government is planning to do in relation to financial markets. (Economic theory is best understood as an ontological reification of capitalist sensitivities represented as natural laws of a construct called 'the economy'.) At critical moments, such as when the Bank of England went off the gold standard in 1931, rather than deploying road-tested knowledge of the 'if, then' kind, central banking relies on the trained intuition of great men and their capacity to make others believe that they know what they're doing, even when they don't. At a university event in London almost a decade after the 2008 crash, Alan Greenspan was remembered by an enthusiastic admirer as having had 'a complete model of the American economy in his body'. Presumably this enabled him always to make the right call, and meant that it was completely unnecessary for him to share his in-the-flesh database-cum-structural equations with the outside world.

Today, central banking's peculiar mix of scientism, intuition, faith healing and showmanship is losing its magic. For years now, central bankers have tried to turn quantitative easing into common sense, even as their friends from finance tell them that 'it cannot go on forever'. But hopes that QE together with zero interest rates would stimulate inflation, insure against deflation, devalue debt and as a result, restore growth, have been dashed. The new key term is 'radical uncertainty', introduced by none other than Mervyn King, former governor of the Bank of England. In his book *The End of Alchemy* (2016), King lets his readers know that 'in a world of radical uncertainty there is no way of identifying the probabilities of future events and no set of equations that describes people's attempts to cope with, rather than optimize against, that uncertainty'. He adds: 'The economic relationships between money, income, saving and interest rates are unpredictable, although they are the outcome of attempts by rational people to cope with an uncertain world.' Operating by scientific or legal rules makes no sense if the real organizing principles of the economy are no longer understood, or if things refuse to be ruled. In such circumstances, even the pretence of control becomes difficult to maintain. According to an email from global investment house PIMCO to its customers in July 2016, most forecasting has become futile because 'the real world is far from stationary' – meaning that, to quote again, 'stuff happens'. 'Structural breaks', the investment house advises, have made it necessary to 'think the unthinkable'. And 'if the future is radically uncertain, the modern central bank practice of giving markets "forward guidance" may be, well, misguided', since it 'creates the illusion that the future is predictable'.

Rising political-economic volatility implies a loss of power for Vogl's central banks, and a loss of respect as well. In July 2017, a year after its embrace of radical uncertainty, the same investment house explained to its clients why interest rates were, and would remain, so low. *Central banks do not figure in the story at all.* Instead the culprit is the 'superstar firm', its rise made possible by new technology and globalized markets. To quote: 'Superstar firms make higher profits, save more than they invest, and pay out a smaller share of their value-added to labour.' This explains 'key macro phenomena such as the global *ex ante* excess of saving over investment, rising income and wealth inequality, and low wage inflation despite falling unemployment, all of which have contributed to the current environment of low natural... and actual interest rates, which in turn supports high valuations for the superstars.'

In this 'winner takes most' world, economic concentration is increasing. Large firms sit on huge cash hoards while labour's income share declines. High wages for the privileged few employed by superstar firms, combined with weak wage pressure in an increasingly fragmented low-wage sector, make for worsening inequality, adding to the global savings glut as 'high-income, wealthy individuals have a higher propensity to save than low-income, less wealthy ones' – an account remarkable for its similarity with standard 'radical' explanations of the crisis of contemporary capitalism.

Together, these dynamics keep inflation down even if central banks want prices to go up. Therefore, the experts say, 'the investment strategy of choice' must be one calibrated to a 'long-term low interest-rate environment'. PIMCO mentions three potential risks for such a strategy: (1) 'A surge in protectionism that leads to accelerating deglobalization'; (2) 'Aggressive antitrust policies that curb superstar firms' quasi-monopoly profits and benefit potential competitors'; and (3) 'a sudden surge in labour's bargaining power'. The investment house considers none of these possibilities likely. But as Greenspan himself noted at an American Enterprise Institute conference in February 2018, under present conditions rates can move in only one direction, upwards, and when they do, they will have devastating consequences for stock prices. The organizer of the event, Desmond Lachman, a former economist at

the IMF, predicted a catastrophic economic and financial crisis in
the near future as a result of rising interest rates.

In a final chapter titled 'Reserves of Sovereignty', Vogl deals
with the submersion of nationally organized financial sectors –
rendered politically unmanageable by financial innovation and the
internationalization of capital – into an emerging global regime.
Here again, Vogl's command of his conceptual apparatus enables
him to make sense of a highly complex process, conceived as yet
another permutation of the relationship between the public and
the private, and amounting to the conversion of 'regulation' into
'governance' – in particular, 'global governance'. Financialization
for Vogl essentially involves the transfer of financial oversight to
the financial markets themselves, ultimately establishing oversight
of states by markets. Subjected to the dictates of capital accumulation, the relations that make up the infrastructure of social life
are financialized, depoliticized and indeed de-socialized. Responsibility for economic order shifts from constitutional, potentially
democratic, governments to 'a patchwork of public entities,
international organizations, treaties and private actors which
superintends the privatization of regulation and, as a consequence,
the marketization and informalization of law and legal institutions'. As governance is privatized, finance becomes the sole
remaining sovereign. 'Global governance', Vogl writes,

> is neither a straightforward liberation of market freedoms nor a
> suppression of state institutions, nor is it a rigid dichotomiza-
> tion of market and state. Since the 1990s, a mutual embedding
> has taken place; permeability has been created, allowing credit
> conditions to dictate the rules of political restructuring. In this
> process, state institutions function as bodies for the anchoring
> of market mechanisms.

Vogl's critics, many of them from the 'public choice' crowd, have
argued that central bank autonomy-cum-supremacy constitutes

the only effective precaution against frivolous democratic politicians recklessly spending their way into office and thereby emptying the public purse. Democratic governments paying for schools and roads are equated with absolutist rulers combating personal boredom by making war. Vogl wastes no time arguing with this. Still, it might have been worth his while to place the evolving relationship between public spending, public debt, taxation and interest, and the public-choice rhetoric surrounding this, in a larger political-economic context transcending institutional analysis proper. What if the pressure for ever-higher public spending was a reflection, not of democratic 'irresponsibility', but of what in Marxian language would be described as a secular tendency toward the 'socialization of production', giving rise to a functional need for private profit-making to be supported by an increasingly elaborate, and correspondingly more expensive, public infrastructure?

It is here that Vogl's institutional analysis of the bipolar world of his zone of indeterminacy might have benefited from being embedded in a political economy of contemporary capitalism, a context in which it would greatly contribute to our understanding of a, shall we say, dialectical 'contradiction' between the limited supply of tax revenue on the one hand – caused by capital's reluctance to be taxed – and on the other, the growing demands, including capitalist demands, for public prepare-and-repair work, from education to environmental clean-up; for public security, from citizen surveillance in the centre to anti-insurgency on the periphery; and for public compensation of citizens for loss of income and status due to capitalist creative destruction. Too little public spending might keep capital away, but too much taxation might have the same effect, while too much public spending would unacceptably narrow the corridor for private profit-making.

Privatization of public provision can, of course, be of help, and has been for some time. But there are limits to it, not least those set by citizen resistance. The remaining option is to finance the growing demands on the state by swelling the public debt – and indeed, if capital must decide between a debt-free tax state and a low-tax debt state, it doesn't find the choice difficult. For under-taxed capital, public debt is a convenient opportunity to lend to the state as private investment what would otherwise be confiscated by the state through taxation. Money lent to the state remains private property, yields interest – at least in normal times – and can be passed on within the family to the next generation. For this to occur, of course, states must be willing and able to service and repay their debt reliably, and it is here that central banks still seem to play an important role in the management of 'financialized' capitalism. Not only can they mediate between states and the financial industry – bankrolling the former and allowing the latter to trade government debt for profit – they also help to keep public debt at a level where states can still be trusted by their private creditors. They do this, for example, by warning the public, with all the authority of their pseudo-scientific theories, about the dangers of excessive government debt – inflation and other maladies – and by advocating a move to balanced budgets through 'austerity' on everything except debt service. Whether this will be enough to close the gap between the maximum taxability of a globally embedded national-capitalist economy, and the rising demands for public infrastructures and services under advanced capitalism, is an open question. It probably falls some distance short, and like privatization, simply postpones the coming clash between private profit-making and its public underwriters.

CHAPTER 3

Chaotic Interregnum

December 2016

NEOLIBERALISM HAS MANY FACETS, and so there is no lack of books on the subject. David Kotz, professor of economics at Amherst, states right at the outset that his perspective is on neoliberal *capitalism*, that is, on the political economy of the beast, leaving its culture and ideology – its Foucauldian as distinguished from its, if you will, Marxian aspect – to others to deal with.* This is fair enough, and indeed Kotz has done an outstanding job within the confines of his remit. His book is well-written, accessible far beyond the economics profession without sacrificing empirical and theoretical precision, and in its first five chapters full of the right kind of data, summarized in well-designed descriptive diagrams of which there are not too many and not too few – excellent material not just for graduate teaching but for the political-economic debate at large.

---

* David M. Kotz, *The Rise and Fall of Neoliberal Capitalism*, Cambridge, MA: Harvard University Press, 2015. For the other side of the coin, see for example Wendy Brown, *Undoing the Demos: Neoliberalism's Stealth Revolution*, Cambridge, MA: MIT Press, 2015; and Gérard Duménil and Dominique Lévy, *Capital Resurgent: Roots of the Neoliberal Revolution*, Cambridge, MA: Harvard University Press, 2004.

As one would expect from someone proudly hailing from the social structure of accumulation school, Kotz places his subject in a historical context, more specifically that of the history of capitalist development, and the narrative he offers reads just right, written true to the spirit of Einstein's famous recipe for good theory, 'Make it simple but not too simple'. Kotz begins with the early liberalism of America's post–Civil War nineteenth century, moving on to the organized capitalism of the Progressive Era and the early neoliberalism of the Roaring Twenties; the state-administered and unionized 'Keynesian' economy of the New Deal and the 'Golden Age'; and the subsequent rise of neoliberalism and its fall in the crash of 2008. History is central to the economics of David Kotz, as it should be but is not in economics in general, and it is framed as a succession of (what else?) social structures of – capitalist – accumulation. Each structure, according to the theory, 'works' for a while but then breaks down from internal conflicts and contradictions, giving way to a new structure bound ultimately to collapse in its turn as well.

Kotz's story is not necessarily new, but it is certainly well told, and with many interesting details. It cannot in any case be told often enough, given the disinformation showered on the public by mainstream economics departments. Kotz adds to received critical wisdom by emphasizing the contribution of trade unions and collective bargaining to post-war democratic capitalism, and generally the significance of the capital-labour relationship during the Golden Age. Kotz also, and justifiably so, spends time and space on the question of why and how the post-war social compromise fell apart in the 1970s. Here he offers useful material for what one could call the defection-of-capital explanation, in particular evidence of the important contribution of organized business in the United States, first to the domestication and then the liberation of capital and capitalism. Kotz associates that shift with a transition from the Committee for Economic Development (CED) to a new organizational form, the Business Roundtable, reconstituting capital as an active political agent after decades of having to serve as an inanimate wealth-creation machine. The role of business interest associations in the American political economy has long been underestimated in comparative politics, and Kotz joins political scientists such as Paul Pierson and Jacob Hacker who have recently begun to remedy this.

The Rise and Fall of Neoliberal Capitalism is about the United States of America. No other country appears, except for a short reference to New Labour and how it continued Thatcher's British transition to neoliberalism, following the example of Clinton and the New Democrats, who continued the work of Reagan. There are reasons for this that should not be taken lightly. The US was and still is the centre of the capitalist world, and the revolt of capital against social democracy began here, making the United States the birthplace of the neoliberal capitalism that culminated in the global crisis of 2008. Without a sufficient understanding of the United States as the engine of contemporary capitalist development, neoliberalism cannot be properly appreciated.

At the same time, being the centre implies a relationship of dominance vis-à-vis a periphery, in the present case with other capitalist or precapitalist countries and regions, from Europe to China, not to forget the raw material supplying regions of Africa and the Middle East. Just as political-economic development in the US and its politics of change and reform will have repercussions on the wider world system, it will be and is affected by that system in turn. Without detracting from Kotz's achievement, widening the scope of social structure of accumulation theory from American to global capitalism seems an urgent task. This would involve figuring in the constraints and opportunities for American capitalism in a global context, including the role of the American military. For example, the financialization of the American economy, detrimental as it has turned out to be for the stability of American capitalism, cannot easily be reversed as long as it is needed to compensate for low competitiveness in other sectors by extracting resources from the rest of the world, including credit to pay for American consumption.[*]

Kotz begins with a summary defining neoliberalism, invoking the usual suspects of globalization, deregulation, welfare cuts, lower minimum wages, reduced marginal tax rates, de-unionization, financialization, fiscal consolidation, etc. Nicely synthesizing two theoretical traditions, Kotz ends up defining neoliberalism as both domination of capital over labour and expansion of market relations into social relations. Chapter 3 recounts the shift from post-war regulated capitalism to post-1980s neoliberal capitalism, paying special attention to the profit squeeze of the 1970s and the subsequent re-orientation of business vis-à-vis organized labour from cooperation to conflict and suppression. Chapter 4 investigates how the neoliberal social structure of accumulation 'worked' economically and socially. In short, while for the economy as a whole it worked less well than regulated capitalism, it worked much better for the rich, at the expense of the poor. Accounting for the economic expansion of the 1990s, Kotz points to an 'interaction among growing inequality, large asset bubbles, and speculatively oriented financial institutions, which together propelled consumption-led growth financed by consumer borrowing', accompanied by low inflation due to de-unionization.

Chapter 5, the longest of the book, reviews the crisis of neoliberalism in 2008 and beyond. Kotz shows how inequality, asset bubbles and speculative finance had given rise to 'three unsustainable trends over the course of the neoliberal era: growing household and financial sector debt ratios, the spread of new toxic financial instruments throughout the financial sector, and increasing excess

---

[*] On how American debt provides for external funding of American internal consumption, see Guido Giacomo Preparata and Domenico D'Amico, 'The Political Economy of Hyper-Modernity: A Tale of America's Hegemonic Exigencies Recounted through the Undulations of the US Balance of Payments, 1946–2015', in Giacomo Preparata, ed., *New Directions for Catholic Social and Political Research: Humanity vs. Hyper-Modernity*, New York: Palgrave Macmillan, 2016.

productive capacity in the real sector of the economy' – trends that ultimately brought the neoliberal accumulation structure to its knees. On the response to the crisis, Kotz argues that while there was initially some fiscal stimulus, it was not enough, which he believes accounts for the sluggishness of the recovery. The 'Keynesian moment' having passed, 'austerity' became the fashion of the day, with unjustified fear of government debt driving a return to pre–Great Depression 'sound money' policies. Kotz blames this for the prolonged stagnation – something on which the last word may not yet have been spoken. Important, in any case, is his account of the high price an entire generation has already paid and is still paying for the failed neoliberal experiment.

Chapters 6 and 7 are exercises in lesson drawing, putting the rise and fall of neoliberalism in the context of history while organizing history in the framework of social structure of accumulation theory. As mentioned, capitalism is held to have gone through five stages, each of which ended in a 'structural crisis . . . followed by major institutional restructuring'. In the process, liberal and regulated accumulation regimes alternated: the first two liberal regimes, the Gilded Age and the Roaring Twenties, were each succeeded by a regulated regime, raising the prospect that this will now repeat itself. Here we note the functionalist character of the theory, its tendency to dwell more on systemic needs than on the political actors required for satisfying them. It is from this vantage point that Kotz's final chapter explores 'possible future paths'; this chapter is easily the book's weakest.

Predictions, as Keynes is said to have said (some say it was Yogi Berra), are always difficult, especially if they are about the future. Kotz is not unaware of this: change, or non-change, he points out, 'will be the outcome of struggles among various groups and classes' which, however, he abstains from specifying. Nevertheless, Kotz sketches out four 'future courses': 'continuation of neoliberal capitalism', 'transition to a business-regulated form of capitalism', 'transition to social democratic capitalism', and 'transition to

democratic-participatory planned socialism' – the final three
being versions of regulated capitalism, their difference consisting
in who will do the regulating: capital (especially finance capital
à la Hilferding), capital and labour, or labour. This menu looks a
little too neat to be true, due perhaps to social structure of accumulation theory positing more or less explicitly that whenever a
social structure of accumulation becomes obsolescent, it must and
therefore will soon be replaced with a more up-to-date successor.
In this it is similar to French *régulation* theory, for which an unreg-
ulated world is inconceivable (although Kotz's 'continuation of
neoliberal capitalism' comes close to such a world). That the next
phase in the history of modern capitalism may be a long period of
chaotic interregnum – an age of indeterminacy – is precluded by
both. Unfortunately, however, this is what may most likely be in
store, due not least to the absence of historical agency strong
enough to re-order a now profoundly disorderly capitalist world, a
condition that Kotz seems implicitly to recognize when he speaks
in all-too-general terms of 'groups and classes'.

Seen from outside the usually optimistic American centre, the
most likely scenario is one in which the United States, the historical host of twentieth-century capitalism, will be too weak to
enforce its own order while remaining strong enough to prevent
others from enforcing theirs. Assuming this to be our future,
Kotz's somewhat pedantic list of the pros and cons of 'democratic-participatory planned socialism' appears more than a little
anachronistic. A brief look at global capitalism's periphery may
make clear what this might mean. In more and more countries –
from Central America to North Africa, the Middle East,
Afghanistan, Pakistan, not to forget the Russian periphery and
Russia itself – the Western model of 'development' has failed, and
so have most local states, typically with the active contribution of
their neoliberal American friends. Millions of people have given
up hope for a better life in their home countries and are on the
move to the United States, *pace* Donald Trump, and Western

Europe, thanks to Angela Merkel. 'Democratic-participatory planned socialism' sounds good, but will there be a *demos* ready to participate in the planning? Will there be stable states maintaining stable institutions for the purpose, and for the implementation of the plan once it has been made? And what is it in the first place that would be planned in Pakistan and Palestine, in Algeria and Afghanistan, in Mali, Mexico and Mississippi, to name just a few?

CHAPTER 4

Modernizing Class Conflict

March 2018

THIS BOOK IS historical-institutionalist political economy at its best.* Obviously it is on industrial relations, but it is also, as it should be, on capitalism and the state, on politics and markets, and most importantly: on their dynamic change over time. Industrial relations – this is one thing that we learn, unless we have already learned it – cannot be understood outside its capitalist-political context, and it must be conceived as a story, a movie not a still, embedded in the long history of modern capitalist society. That history, quite appropriately, can be recounted as one of 'modernization', but not in the 1950s and 1960s American sense where it stands for quiet, steady, universal and basically self-driven development towards ever higher levels of prosperity, democracy, and general happiness. Rather, what Amable identifies as 'modernization' is a political project of a state under capitalism trying to design a regime that overcomes the dysfunctions of liberalism while avoiding the lure of socialism or communism – a perennial political search for a 'Third Way'

---

* Bruno Amable, *Structural Crisis and Institutional Change in Modern Capitalism: French Capitalism in Transition*, Oxford: Oxford University Press, 2017.

and for a political coalition capable of sustaining it that goes back to the beginning of capitalist industrialization in the nineteenth century.

Amable's narrative proceeds on a number of theoretical premises that are worth extracting. A state in a capitalist society is more than just an 'executive committee of the bourgeoisie'; it requires and sometimes achieves a considerable amount of creativity in cobbling together what Amable calls a 'dominant social bloc' – a coalition of forces capable of securing both social peace, or at least social acquiescence, and successful accumulation of capital. All such alignments are precarious; they can and do collapse in political-economic crises when the balancing act between pacification and accumulation goes wrong, for external or internal reasons – for example, technological change, foreign competitive pressure, or erosion of bloc solidarity and political support. Capitalist societies, Amable suggests, never rest: they continuously produce social discontent rooted in what ultimately are fundamental incompatibilities between individual and collective desires for a good life and the functional requirements of profit-making in competitive markets. States undertaking to govern a capitalist society must moderate the conflict between the two, among other things by setting up effective institutions regulating the capital-labour relationship, which is where surplus value is ultimately generated. The institutionalization of what we call industrial relations and its continuous revision in response to changing circumstances is an important part of this exercise and, inevitably, one of the central issues on the agenda of any government seeking to make capitalism acceptable to society and society acceptable to capitalism.

The focus of Amable's book is France, but the general lessons that can be gleaned from it are essential for any up-to-date theory of capitalism and capitalist political economy. French bourgeois society felt from early on that laissez-faire liberalism was not enough to secure working class compliance with the exigencies of capitalist progress. It understood that it needed a state with the capacity to steer the country through the narrow passage between the Scylla of a self-regulating market (Polanyi) and the Charybdis of socialism and communism. 'Modernist' experiments included state planning, corporatism – remember the preface to the second edition of Durkheim's *Division du travail* – and the 'post-war settlement' of Fordist mass production and consumption. All of these served their purpose more or less well, but after a while they had run their course and had to be replaced with other, more timely, but equally temporary solutions. Amable, one of the main contributors to the literature on 'varieties of capitalism', has framed what is a single case history in concepts so clear and sophisticated that readers interested in and knowledgeable about other capitalist countries will find it easy to recognize differences and similarities and derive general insights from them.

Among the many merits of Amable's study is that it reminds us of the centrality of the wage nexus for the politics of capitalist democracies. Capitalism is about what Marx calls *Plusmacherei* (the making of a surplus) that can be invested to yield more surplus, in unending progress. Employment, productivity, prosperity may as side-effects ensue; or they may not, and this is perfectly fine as long as profit is forthcoming and society can be kept compliant. Profit arises where labour power is successfully deployed to work old capital so that new capital can be formed. When profits are squeezed, for whatever reason, as they were at the end of the Fordist period in the 1970s, the time has come for the next round of 'modernization'. Then a new social compact needs to be forged – another social bloc able to achieve dominance – that is able to deliver wage moderation, 'flexibility' of employment, pension cuts, a higher retirement age, privatization of public services, etc. Preferably profit-enhancing 'reforms' of this sort are to be delivered democratically, with the agreement of a political majority concerned about national competitiveness and jobs migrating abroad, about restoring growth, defending the work ethic, or bringing 'outsiders' back in. But it must also be possible, if need be, for democracy to be suspended, for example, by contracting-in reforms as international obligations, or delegating economic policy to technocratic institutions such as central banks or international monetary funds.

Note that the 'cutting' – the squeezing of labour – that is in this way administered is open-ended, as profits can never be too high for those who depend on them. Labour regimes can always be improved by cutting and more cutting, relative and absolute, as long as subsequent socialist temptations can be suppressed. This is the hard core of capitalist political economy, with all sorts of 'narratives' constructed to allow governments to accommodate the systemic constraint of surplus-making, and a huge list of parameters to work on: competition, 'globalization', immigration, privatization, credit and debt, family structures, education and, of course, labour law and industrial relations in a narrow sense. Capitalists are uniquely creative, or creatively destructive, when it comes to inventing new ways of extracting surplus from the labour process and putting together a social bloc to oversee the capitalist game as long as it lasts.

There is no guarantee, however, that the balancing act between capitalism and social life, as demanded of the capitalist state, will always be successful. In fact, Amable's history of political conflict and its regulation in France shows that the shelf life of capital-friendly settlements was never long and has recently become even shorter. Amable traces how economic doctrines, political strategies and social alliances took turns as French nationalist-bourgeois ambitions to rise to international capitalist leadership and compete on an equal footing with the US and Germany remained unfulfilled. By the end of the *trente glorieuses* a hectic search had begun for a new formula, political and economic, to 'modernize' French capitalism without either pulverizing society or suffocating the market. In the process, the two big centrist parties of the post-war era, the Gaullists and the Socialists, moved ever closer to each other, until they became practically indistinguishable. (There is an exciting parallel here to other European countries, like Germany and the UK, that Amable might have wanted to emphasize a little more.) The book recounts how in the early 1980s Mitterrand and his Socialist government, in their desperate effort to domesticate their unruly society, discovered 'Europe' and the project of a common, German-style currency as a means to import German-style economic discipline into France. Increasingly they realized, however, that the cure they had in mind to enhance French 'competitiveness' was impossible to administer with democratic participation. Effectively this left the bottom-up articulation of protest to a new right-wing party, the Front National (FN) of the Le Pens. Later, two conservative presidents, Chirac and Sarkozy, equally failed to overcome popular resistance against 'flexibility' and austerity and break what bourgeois opinion considered an economic and political deadlock. When Hollande defeated Sarkozy in 2012, returning the Socialists to power, it soon became clear that they lacked any idea, independent or not, of how to assemble a 'reform'-minded social bloc, left or right, that would be capable, again, of 'modernizing' the country. In the end Hollande, having become an object of popular derision, abstained from seeking a second term.

Amable's account ends shortly before Macron's rise to power from the ashes of a bankrupt party system. But the historical lines he draws in his book make this outcome appear, sooner or later, as inevitable. After democracy, Bonapartism, of a new sort: peddled to the masses by the well-oiled public relations machinery of French financial capitalism, promoted by a synthetic make-believe party created out of the blue to disguise what is in fact the personal rule of a creature of Hollande, whom he stabbed in the back when he saw close-up how shallow and burned-out he was. The first thing Macron did in office was push through by decree another 'reform' of the French labour code, no longer primarily to revitalize French capitalism – nobody believes that it can do this – but to oblige the Germans, in particular Angela Merkel, to reciprocate with 'European solidarity', meaning increased investment, higher debt ceilings, and fiscal support. 'Modernization' under Macron is, more than under any of his predecessors, identified with 'Europe', the ersatz ideology of his presidency. This was not good enough, however, to sustain the hype; in the fall of 2017 Macron's approval ratings are lower than those of any French president at this early time of his term. Freely dished-out advice to the unemployed, according to which 'the best way to get a suit is by getting a job', or public musings on railway stations as places where 'successful people meet people who are nothing', have reminded the public of Macron's upper-class descent and make it apparent that he had never had to 'press the flesh' as normal politicians have to. Soon people, and Macron himself, may also remember that if only a few votes in the first round of the 2017 presidential election had been cast differently, it would have been the candidate of the radical Left – the Socialists ended up with less than 5 per cent – who would have faced, and certainly defeated, Le Pen in the run-off (just as Sanders, had he been allowed to win the Democratic primaries, could have run against Trump, likely defeating him). The story of capitalism and the twists and turns of the politics of its discontents, this is to say – so masterfully reconstructed in its French version by Bruno Amable – is far from over, in France and everywhere else.

CHAPTER 5

The German Recipe

May 2017

H OW COULD GERMANY, of all countries, become a paragon of politically stable and economically successful democratic capitalism in the 1970s (*Modell Deutschland*) and later, in the 2000s, Europe's uncontested economic and political superpower? Accounting for this requires recourse to the Braudelian *longue durée*, in which apparently utter devastation may turn into a lasting blessing – and where in the context of capitalist development, destruction can be progress because capitalist progress *is* destruction, of a more or less creative sort. In 1945, unconditional surrender forced Germany – more precisely, its Western part and what was left of it – into a 'second round of capitalist transformation', in Perry Anderson's apt expression, like no other European country has had to undergo up to the present day.* Germany's 'second round' was a violent, sharp and short push forward into social and economic 'modernity', driving it forever from the halfway house of Weimar. It was a painful dismantling of social and political structures of domination and solidarity that had, as 'feudal fetters', held back the country's capitalist progress – structures that continue

---

* Perry Anderson, 'The Heirs of Gramsci', *New Left Review*, no. 100, 2016, p. 75.

in locally different manifestations to block capitalist rationaliza-
tion in so many other European countries.*

At the top of the list of the transformative events that put West
Germany on track to what it was to become is the arrival of 10
million refugees-expellees from the East, in the end making up
roughly one in five inhabitants of a devastated territory less than
half the size of the pre-war Reich. While some of them remained
isolated, depressed and poor for the rest of their lives, others had
brought with them as their only possession a resolute determination to fit in and be a success in what was for them almost a
foreign country. As they settled down, literally where the trains
from the East had spewed them out, they forever disrupted the
fabric of a still largely traditional society divided between urban
and rural, Catholic and Protestant, Left and Right. Centuries-old
parochial ways of life and socio-cultural milieus were broken up,
often against adamant resistance – until the newcomers had found
their place, contributing their skills and hard work to their new
homeland and forcing the locals to allow them a chance to estab-
lish themselves in a society that had, by their arrival, become more
competitive and meritocratic than ever.

This was far from all. As Ralf Dahrendorf was probably the first
to recognize in its full significance, in the new Federal Republic
the two social and political forces that had between them worn
down the Weimar Republic: the Eastern aristocracy – the *Junker*
which already Max Weber had identified as the *Reich*'s main roadblock to capitalist modernity – and the Communists of the
Comintern, were no longer present.† The former had been deci-
mated by the Nazis after the putsch of 1944, and what was left of
them had been killed or driven from their estates by the Soviets

---

*   Albert Hirschman, 'Rival Interpretations of Market Society: Civilizing,
Destructive, or Feeble?', *Journal of Economic Literature*, vol. 20, no. 4, 1982, pp.
1463–84.

†   Ralf Dahrendorf, *Gesellschaft und Demokratie in Deutschland*, Munich:
Piper, 1965.

with the advance of the Red Army. The Communists, for their part, now had their own state under Soviet sponsorship, the German Democratic Republic, which so much weakened them in the West that in 1956 the Constitutional Court was able to outlaw their party. This eliminated almost in one stroke both wings of the anti-capitalist 'countermovement' (Polanyi), the reactionary as well as the potentially progressive one, leaving only the Social Democrats (SPD) on the centre-left and the Christian Democrats (CDU) on the centre-right. The latter, while grown out of Weimar's Catholic *Zentrumspartei*, appealed to Christians generally, reflecting the post-war break-up of homogenous religious local communities. Add to this the disappearance of the Nazis as an organized political force and the incarceration of Germany's industrial tycoons by the Allies (soon of course to be released to help with the Korean War), and you see a vastly simplified political landscape, located in an economic geography shorn of the economically parasitic manorial feudalism of the former Prussia. Instead it was dominated by what was to become a highly productive dualism between the small-firm economy of the South, the Southwest and the Rhineland on the one hand, and on the other hand the huge industrial complexes, especially in the Ruhr Valley (whose owners had been kept in custody long enough for the British to introduce strong rights for unions and workforces to participate in the management particularly of coal and steel companies).

Relative to the new structural fundamentals, the influence of ordoliberalism on the German political economy tends to be vastly overestimated. An offspring of Protestant social theory, it had to exist side by side with a born-again Rhenish-Catholic corporatism, which was soon to blend indistinguishably into the class corporatism of a no longer politically divided union movement.* Germany was never ordoliberal, if this is to mean the

---

* On this and the following, see Philip Manow, 'Ordoliberalismus als ökonomische Ordnungstheologie', *Leviathan*, vol. 29, no. 2, 2001, pp. 179–98. Less specific, but in

elimination of unions, collective bargaining, or worker participation on the shop floor and on management boards – the authoritarian liberalism of Carl Schmitt in the early 1930s. Reducing the role of the state in the economy to something like indirect control was a widely shared objective after the Nazi dictatorship; but this did not mean that capital would be given free reign, or that the distribution of incomes and wealth would be left to the market. Ordoliberalism's discovery of competition as an instrument to keep market power in check was applied solely to product markets, never to labour markets, and only much later to markets for capital; it was therefore appreciated even by trade unionists and Social Democrats. Catholics, empowered by the new economic and political geography, with their concern with 'social justice' – a concept someone like Hayek considered outright nonsensical – always regarded ordoliberalism, ensconced in Ludwig Erhard's Economics Ministry, with suspicion. This was so even though its standard-bearers adopted the rhetoric of the 'social market economy' and committed themselves to a distributional objective like 'prosperity for all' (*Wohlstand für alle*). In any case, Adenauer, Rhenish Catholic that he was, knew the pacifying capacity of social policy well and skilfully used the Ministry of Labour, with its ingrained Weimar SPD and Centre Party tradition, to ensure that ordoliberalism never became the only game in town and had to live in a delicate balance of power with strong forces of 'social justice'.*

Unconditional surrender and the subsequent carving up of the Reich helped the German economy in yet another way. German

---

English, is Manow, 'Modell Deutschland as an Interdenominational Compromise', Harvard University Center for European Studies Working Papers, no. 3, 2000.

* Even with respect to competition policies and anti-trust legislation, ordoliberalism suffered painful setbacks in the politics of West Germany. In response, its leading theorists in economics and economic law early on shifted their activities to the emerging European Economic Community, whose competition law they managed effectively to monopolize, due to lack of competition.

industry had always been dependent on foreign markets for both manufactured goods and raw materials. Being denied access to them, especially by the British, was an old German nightmare, one that the Nazis tried to end through imperial conquest and autarky. For the small, wholly defeated, semi-sovereign West Germany, this had forever ceased to be an option. Integration into the American-led Bretton Woods free trade regime, and later into the European Economic Community, offered a much superior alternative, especially as it included fixed exchange rates under which the new West German currency became increasingly undervalued over time. In the 1950s and 1960s, this laid the foundation for the re-establishment of a uniquely strong, heavily export-dependent industrial sector which, continuing older traditions, was to become the centre of gravity of the West German and later the German political economy.

Werner Plumpe's book, unfortunately, does not quite deliver what its title promises.* Rather than a continuous historical narrative over two centuries, it offers twelve chapters on selected subjects, originally written and previously published in German, mostly between 2001 and 2009 (two chapters are from 2013). While the translation is sometimes awkward, the collection does cover interesting and important facets of German economic history, with a focus on firms, business associations and industrial relations. Synthesizing Plumpe's chapters, one finds strong support of a view of the German economy as export-heavy and export-dependent; see in particular chapter 10, which gives an informative account especially of the postwar *Wirtschaftswunder* and the structural changes that followed, with occasional comparisons with the GDR (a chapter that would have deserved better language editing). Moreover, as far as this reader remembers, Plumpe does not even mention ordoliberalism. Instead, he rightly devotes much

---

* Werner Plumpe, *German Economic and Business History in the 19th and 20th Centuries*, London: Palgrave Macmillan, 2016.

space to the German tradition of 'social partnership',* which he grounds in a shared interest of capital and labour in industrial success in foreign markets. Here Plumpe comes close to a historical political economy of German capitalism, showing in several chapters that a desire for cross-class cooperation and social compromise existed among German employers even during the Weimar Republic. This argues against a leftist mainstream that locates German business during the interwar years firmly on the side of anti-unionism and indeed fascism. Plumpe's revisionism even includes occasional expressions of sympathy for free market liberalism and 'flexible labour markets', a scepticism against the social-democratic solution to the class conflict unexpected of someone who until 1989 was a member of the (West) German Communist Party, the DKP.†

More than is assumed by outside observers to be a collective memory of the hyper-inflation of the 1920s, it is Germany's structural condition as an over-industrialized national economy that accounts for the deep aversion to inflation that has pervaded German economic policy since the *Währungsreform* of 1948. That the West German central bank, the Bundesbank, was from its beginning strictly independent from the West German government came in handy even to the SPD when it was in government in the 1970s. But that had less to do with ordoliberalism than with the fact that the introduction of the D-Mark preceded the foundation of the West German state – not to mention the Allies, who wanted to prevent future German governments from financing

---

* That is, between unions and employers. The concept is genuinely alien to the Anglophone world. Years ago the author used it in a lecture he gave to a lay audience in London. One of the listeners asked for a different term since for him, 'social partnership' meant attending parties and receptions together without being otherwise related.

† In this respect, the book's final chapter about labour relations in the former GDR and how they contributed to its demise – a subject as yet hardly addressed by economic historians and political economists – offers informative reading.

future rounds of rearmament through the printing press. Shared interests in low inflation also informed the West German class compromise, with the metal workers' union, IG Metall, soon dominating the country's industrial relations. The accumulating trade surplus that ensued motivated the revaluation of the D-Mark in 1969 by the incoming Social-Liberal government, in an attempt to shift economic growth from foreign trade to domestic demand. Like subsequent revaluations under post–Bretton Woods floating exchange rates, this worked only temporarily due to what economists call a J-curve effect: even then, German exports were not very price-sensitive, apparently because of their superior quality. Still, employment in manufacturing declined, slowly but steadily, and in 1984 IG Metall tried to stop this through a six-week nationwide strike for a thirty-five -hour workweek. This was the first time that the *Economist* and similar quality papers saw Germany as going under from 'Eurosclerosis'.

Nevertheless, by the end of the 1980s, with a population half the size of Japan's and a quarter that of the United States, Germany had surpassed both countries as *Exportweltmeister*. Underlying this was a move of West German industry into high-value-added global market segments where competition was over quality and service rather than price, a restructuring process accommodating, and even forced by, powerful trade unions and works councils defending high wages and a compressed wage structure. Upmarket restructuring drew on longstanding German traditions of quality engineering and vocational training (on the latter, see Kathleen Thelen, *How Institutions Evolve*, 2004), both continuously upgraded since the educational reforms of the 1960s and 1970s. What resulted was a pattern political economists called diversified quality production (DQP), reflecting a national supply-side strategy that utilized traditional cultural and institutional resources for a rewriting of the class compromise, in the workplace as well as in the political economy at large, that built on and defended the strong manufacturing sector inherited from the early post-war decades, at a time when in other countries deindustrialization had already progressed quite far.

Path-dependency continued to govern the story – a story that Plumpe unfortunately ceases to tell as early as the beginning of the 1990s. German unification was followed by a deep recession, not least because the oversized West German manufacturing sector had no need for additional production sites in the *Neue Länder*. Rapidly increasing nonwage labour costs, due to Kohl's decision to impose the costs of unification on the social security system rather than the taxpayer, resulted in high and rising unemployment. This inspired public debates on whether Germany had, in the 1980s, missed the move towards a 'service economy' on the British and US models (although arguably the 1:1 currency union with the East was more to blame than anything else – a lesson that was apparently lost when another monetary union, this time at European level, was instituted). Again, the *Economist* and the *Financial Times* nominated Germany for 'the sick man of Europe'. As 'globalization' opened up possibilities for employers to relocate production and employment to Eastern Europe and China in particular, IG Metall in 1995 urged the Kohl government and the employers to form a tripartite 'Alliance for Jobs'; this, however, was obstructed by the Liberal Party (FDP) and the CDU floor leader, Wolfgang Schäuble, who preferred 'structural reforms' (as he would two decades later in the Mediterranean). In the years that followed, unions in the exposed sector of the German economy learned the hard way to accept wage restraint without compensation, in a painful process that extended from a fruitless second attempt at a tripartite employment policy under Schröder (1998–99) to the Agenda 2010 (starting in 2003) and the first Merkel government (2005–09) – after Merkel had threatened to curtail, through legislation, the right of trade unions to collective bargaining at the sectoral level and delegate wage-setting to firm-level works councils.

As with unification, one regrets that Plumpe's essays never touch on the EMU; both still await inclusion in a long-term historical perspective on the German political economy. In the rapidly internationalizing economy of the 2000s, employment in a manufacturing country such as Germany depended more than ever on international 'competitiveness', not just in product but also in labour markets, since manufacturing jobs are easier than service sector jobs to relocate abroad. Keeping inflation and unit labour costs low became the unions' overriding concern, again making them reliable allies of employers and the government. Still, although German wage-setting institutions were gradually recalibrated in response to political and employer pressures, this did not help much at first. With the transition to a single interest rate for the whole of Euroland, Germany as a low-inflation country had to live with interest rates higher than it would have needed for monetary stability, whereas the high-inflation member countries benefited, if only for a while, from rates too low for them. Gradually, however, rising unit labour costs in the more inflationary member countries (which under the EMU could no longer defend themselves through devaluation) and constant or even declining unit labour costs in Germany turned the table. After 2008, when credit for the countries with lagging 'competitiveness' was no longer forthcoming, Germany finally experienced its second *Wirtschaftswunder* while the economies of the Mediterranean EMU member countries began to collapse.

It is here that David Audretsch and Erik Lehman pick up the thread.[*] How did Germany manage to muster, according to their book's subtitle, 'economic resilience in an era of global turbulence', rising from its deathbed in the 1990s to global economic predominance after 2008? The explanation, according to the authors, is 'seven secrets' that they set out to reveal in seven chapters: (1) lots of small firms (*Mittelstand*) with a new spirit of entrepreneurship

---

[*]   David B. Audretsch and Erik E. Lehmann, *The Seven Secrets of Germany: Economic Resilience in an Era of Global Turbulence*, Oxford and New York: Oxford University Press, 2016.

prompted by Schröder branding 2004 the 'Year of Innovation'; (2) more university students and higher spending on research and education, and German universities liberating themselves from 'the weight of the ponderous centuries-old model of the university crafted by Humboldt'; (3) regional development policies ('*Ordnungspolitik*', it is astonishingly claimed, 'provides the legal mandate for the government to undertake *Standortpolitik* and engage in politics to enhance competitiveness and economic performance'); (4) a superior physical infrastructure; (5) 'flexibility' in combining 'laptops with lederhosen', meaning innovation with tradition; (6) a high rate of innovation, in particular in manufacturing; (7) feeling good again about being German. Five of the seven, of course, are of long standing and already existed before and during the slump of the 1990s; Schröder's 'Year of Innovation' was soon forgotten; the expansion of tertiary education collides with the vocational training system that Audretsch and Lehman rightly mention as an important institutional resource; and as to the seventh secret, look at the evidence supplied.

Audretsch and Lehman account for short-term variation predominantly through long-term constants. The 'resilience' of the German economy before 1990 is not even mentioned, nor is the contribution of unification, globalization and the two monetary unions, German and European, to the crisis of the 1990s and early 2000s. Historical-institutionalist analysis is overlaid by culturalist speculation based on national clichés as found in newspaper stories and the utterances of popstars like David Bowie and Ashton Kutcher (who is reported to have made a million-dollar investment in a Berlin 'start-up' run by an American Wellesley graduate appropriately named Caitlin Winner). What results when economists venture into 'culture' is a book that makes the reader cringe on almost every page, forcing her to make hard choices between laughing and crying. Comparatively minor blunders – the *Kreditanstalt für Wiederaufbau* becomes the *Kreditanstalt für Weiterentwicklung*, and we encounter 'the American

playwright Henry Miller' – set the stage for exercises in cultural-
ism that even the most talented satirist could not top. A small
selection from the chapter titled '(Infra)Structure':

> What do most Americans want to pass along to the next gener-
> ation? Freedom . . . But Germany is different. Of course
> Germans value freedom . . . But Germans also value something
> else highly – beauty. German culture and sensibilities are a
> descendant of classical Greek values – which appreciate and
> hold beauty to rank among the greatest values . . . In Germany,
> beauty is embedded in a sense of structure. Consider the most
> compelling music ever composed in Germany, the national
> treasure of the great classical composers. Where would the
> beauty of Beethoven, Handel, Bach or Wagner be without
> structure? . . . If German is the language of classical music, with
> its heavily imposing structures, the Romance languages are
> better characterized by jazz, with its spontaneity, inspiration,
> and free format . . .

And so on. The high points are reached when the authors freely (as
Americans?) make up German words for German cultural habits or
practices they claim to have observed. The biggest howler appears
in chapter 8 dealing with Secret No. 7: Germany's final recovery
from its obsession with its Nazi past, as witnessed by Audretsch and
Lehman during the football world championship of 2006 (an event
to which they return again and again with untiring passion). Up
until then, we learn, Germans were given to *Versonnenheit*, translated by the authors as 'atonement', a behaviour alleged to have
prevented non-Germans from participating in the German economy. Being a fan of the German language, I swear that I have never
heard this word used, nor any of its (few) cognates, anywhere near
the context in which it appears in this book. To make sure, I
consulted the *Duden* and found *versonnen*, an adjective meaning
lost in thought, dreaming, forgetful of the world, smiling.

Returning to the sources of contemporary German economic success, the historical dependence of German prosperity on the export of manufactured goods and, later, the non-export of manufacturing jobs, explains why appeals to German unions to help rectify the obscene trade imbalance between Germany and other euro countries by demanding higher wages, and thereby raising unit labour costs, cannot but fall on deaf ears. For German industrial unions, the euro is the ideal solution for the employment problem that hit them in the 1990s with the return of price competition and the internationalization of production systems. The EMU gives German manufacturing a captive market in Europe, plus a secure competitive edge over European competitors that have to operate in more inflationary institutional settings. On top of it all, it equips them with an undervalued currency in markets outside Euroland, especially today as the ECB's 'quantitative easing' keeps inflating the euro money supply. Saving the EMU by containing the competitiveness of their industry, as is sometimes suggested to German unions by outside observers, would for them amount to committing suicide for fear of death.* It would also break up their tripartite alliance with employers and the government, a class-collaborative transformation of the post-war class compromise held together, no longer by trade union power, but by the constraints and opportunities of the EMU and a shared fundamental interest in German international competitiveness.

As indicated, it is not only the unions for whom the competitiveness of German manufacturing is paramount. Their priorities are also those of the government – which currently is a Grand Coalition formed of the centre right, representing industry, and the centre left, where the SPD is basically the political arm of IG

---

* See the utter failure of all attempts at 'wage coordination' among European trade unions, in spite of unending programmatic commitments and declarations of good intentions.

Metall. Trying to explain Germany's behaviour in the euro crisis to a non-German audience, Franz-Josef Meiers, like Audretsch and Lehmann, puts his theoretical money on culture instead of structure, blaming what he considers a disastrous tragicomedy of errors on Merkel's and the whole country's supposed religious adherence to the prescriptions of – guess what? – Ordoliberalism.* In this he outs himself as a true believer in Anglo-American neo-Keynesian doctrine, from Paul Krugman to Martin Wolf, which he unquestioningly regards as a universal wellspring of generally valid and easily applicable recipes for economic recovery. Unlike Audretsch and Lehman, Meiers knows and respects the rules of scholarly craftsmanship. His message is simple: all it takes for Euroland to flourish is Angela Merkel, and she alone, shedding the mindset of the 'Swabian housewife' (Meiers, as a devoted culturalist, is never afraid of clichés) to end 'austerity', start borrowing and spending and allow other countries to do the same, so that eventually everybody in Europe will be better off and live happily ever after.

Is Merkel, is Germany, in their refusal to do the neo-Keynesian right thing, mad or bad? Meiers does not pay heed to the fact that the German economy, including the German labour market, is today doing better than ever in the last thirty years, *with* austerity, budget balancing, zero inflation, and government deleveraging. The reason, he believes, why Germany rejects Europe-wide debt mutualization or debt forgiveness, public deficits at home and abroad, and higher unit labour costs in Germany to get 'Europe' going again is that ordoliberalism comes with sado-monetarism: with *Schadenfreude* about the sinners having to pay for their trespasses with their suffering. While this would indicate badness, Meiers also seems to believe that German austerity preferences reflect mad short-sightedness: an inability to see that what benefits 'the Germans' now, at the expense of others, will later in some

---

* Franz-Josef Meiers, *Germany's Role in the Euro Crisis: Berlin's Quest for a More Perfect Monetary Union*, Cham: Springer, 2015.

unspecified way do damage to them as well. This would point not to a moral but to a cognitive deficiency – Merkel needing to be enlightened by neo-Keynesian scientific authorities. Perhaps Germans are bad and mad at the same time: does their Protestant-ordoliberal desire to punish prevent them from understanding their own interests?

For Meiers, that the euro has turned out to be the ideal solution to the structural problems of a national economy whose prosperity depends on the export performance of an oversized manufacturing sector seems not worth much thought. Nor does he consider the possibility that countries that, unlike Germany, require a soft currency to thrive would be better off outside the euro, in a flexible European monetary regime allowing them to restore their 'competitiveness' by way of occasional devaluations against hard-currency Germany. Here Meiers is no less dogmatic than Merkel with her mantra, 'If the euro fails, Europe fails' – although lacking a structural perspective, he fails to comprehend its deeper meaning. 'Germany's role in the euro crisis', *pace* Meiers, is informed by the country's national economic interest as sellable to a German electorate, as well as by the constraints and opportunities inherent in the, for all practical purposes, unchangeable institutional framework of the EMU – a monetary union without a political union. Meiers and those sharing his views expect the German state to act as though the political union that the German government of the 1990s had wanted to come with monetary union had not been blocked by France and other countries insisting, and continuing to insist, on their national sovereignty. That the EMU is structured as it is, emphasizing individual-national 'responsibility' and lacking provisions for international 'solidarity', is not so much 'ordoliberal' as it is, by and large, the only way a monetary union between otherwise sovereign states can exist.

Meiers believes that the disease of the eurozone can be cured by a democratically elected German government acting as *ideeller Gesamteuropäer* and voluntarily sacrificing some of the national 'competitiveness' that monetary union has bestowed on the German economy – despite our living in a world of neoliberal capitalism, where it is clearly 'not from the benevolence of the butcher' that anyone can 'expect [their] dinner', but only, if at all, from others following 'their own self-interest'. Similarly stark assumptions that Meiers makes without ever examining them include that, in an era of secular stagnation, it is possible to restart growth by further adding to public debt, although for decades now public debt has increased alongside declining growth; that growth in the Eurozone would, or could, by means of a common regional policy, be equally distributed among countries, reversing a long-standing trend of growing inequality; that all Eurozone countries respond equally to fiscal stimulus, and that increased public spending in Germany would somehow increase employment in Italy or Spain; that all Euroland countries follow the same growth model (although we are now beginning to learn that in some countries growth is domestic demand-driven while in others it is driven by export profits – see Lucio Baccaro and Chris Howell, *Trajectories of Neoliberal Transformation* (2017); or that debt relief for over-indebted countries would solve their underlying competitiveness problems, which derive from a social contract that requires a minimum level of inflation to be in equilibrium (unlike Germany, where inflation would undermine the social contract).

Can Germany, given the uncertainties of today's global capitalism, the country's critical need for monetary stability and competitive advantage, and its small size relative to the United States of the 1950s and 1960s, really be accused of not acting as a 'responsible' European hegemon? In my view, what Germany might rightly be accused of is its insistence on the euro, and its reckless identification of the common currency with 'the European project'. Here, of course, the governments of France and the Mediterranean countries are to blame as well, as they still hope to use the hard euro as an external constraint – a *vincolo esterno* – with which to 'modernize' their unruly political economies (and perhaps in the process extract a little help from their German friends). With the EMU instituted as it is, and the path to political union foreclosed, not only by the states but also by their peoples, the Merkel government, as would any other German government, has only one recipe to offer Europe: that its countries, each for itself, catch up with German competitiveness by subjecting themselves to their own 'second round of capitalist transformation' through what is called 'structural reforms' in the technocratic jargon of the day – meaning the replacement of traditional forms of social solidarity with competition and, perhaps later, the embedding of competition in modern, formally institutionalized, political forms of solidarity. For this, willing governments must be kept in power, if need be through more or less subtle ways of suspending democracy, all the more so since resistance to the treatment is growing on a broad front. Here, as so often in her long career, Merkel is anything but dogmatic, and certainly not beholden to ordoliberal orthodoxy, given that what is at stake is Germany's most precious historical achievement, secure access to foreign markets at a low and stable exchange rate. For several years now, the German government under Merkel has allowed the ECB under Draghi and the European Commission under Juncker to invent and apply the most devious methods to circumvent the Maastricht treaties, from financing government deficits to subsidizing ailing banks.* Needless to say that none of this did anything to resolve the underlying structural problems of the Eurozone. Up until now, however, it did what it was supposed to do: buy time from election to election for supportive 'reform' governments in European countries, and for Germany to enjoy yet another year of prosperity.

---

* For a scathing critique from what is a truly neoliberal-ordoliberal perspective on Merkel's connivance (*'plan- und ideenlos'*) with the ever more adventurous European rescue operations, see Johannes Becker and Clemens Fuest, 'Planloser Hegemon: Deutschlands Rolle in der EU', *Frankfurter Allgemeine Zeitung*, 1 December 2016. See also, by the same authors, *Der Odysseus-Komplex*, discussed in chapter 9.

PART II

Democracy

CHAPTER 6

The Custard and the Wall

March 2019

W HAT A STRANGE BOOK – strange but indispensable nevertheless.* Varoufakis's account of his 'battle
with Europe's deep establishment' drips with sentimentality. Too obvious are the traces left by the helping hand of
American specialists in the art of turning an all-too-serious book
into a bestseller. Most important to them: make the bearer of bad
news and the narrator of excessive detail appear as human as
humanly possible. So whenever the uninitiated might want to put
the book aside, exhausted and wondering why they should know
all this, we get home stories galore: marital bliss with a reliably
supportive good wife, Danae; dinners with friends; memories
from the old student days; controversial-but-not-too controversial
debates with teenage daughters; surprise encounters with random
poor or with German secret service agents who urged the hero to
continue fighting the good fight. In between, as is not unusual in
memoirs, the hero always knows what is to be done – had everybody listened to him, Europe would now be one great prosperous

---

* Yanis Varoufakis, *Adults in the Room: My Battle with Europe's Deep
Establishment*, London: Bodley Head, 2017.

democratic republic – and if he makes a mistake this it is because he is too trusting, too naïve for the intrigues both abroad and at the court of Tsipras, a Parsifal or Siegfried out of the woods of the University of Texas in Austin, where good faith was all that was needed for a good life.

And yet: indispensable. For whom? For the quality journalists working for the quality press – who will, however, have no time for a book of this length and are in any case all set to gainfully carry on producing the fake reporting by which they helped the masters of 'Europe' get rid of that bizarre Don Quixote from Brussels' Greek colony. Also for the armies of useless European functionaries busy spinning self-aggrandizing stories in which they have important things to say and decide, until they are soon moved on to some other bureaucratic bullshit job – but they don't read books, not because they have no time (they have a lot of it) but as a matter of principle. Certainly, one would think, for the legions of teachers and students of 'policy science', untiringly working to think up 'strategies' for 'problem solving' to be entrusted to 'decision-makers' thirsty for 'fresh ideas' – although if they read the book and managed not to suppress its insights in psychological self-defence, they might look for another occupation, one with customers that exist not only in their fantasies.

Where Varoufakis's book is more than just your usual, often inevitably self-indulgent memoir, it provides a merciless phenom-enology of how our world is governed in this era of post-democratic neoliberalism, a field report highly plausible to everyone who has ever tried to make sense of today's political goings-on without fall-ing victim to the secret charm of political power. What Varoufakis describes in admirable detail is a politics of astonishingly disor-ganized irresponsibility– a big mush, one sideshow after the next, a parade of drifting busybodies and stuffed shirts, making senseless decisions in senseless meetings, or no decisions at all – sitting and wobbling on top of a deep substructure cast in armoured concrete and entirely beyond its reach. 'Try to nail a pudding to the wall!', the floor leader of the German SPD once famously shouted in a debate with the then chancellor, Ludwig Erhard – but in Europe the pudding is not a person but a system. In his tour from capital to capital, office to office, conference room to conference room, Varoufakis encounters many nice people; the tone is pleasant, sympathy is expressed with the plight of the Greeks, even support – until he hits the underlying concrete and an executioner is called in, a Jeroen Dijsselbloem, for example, speaking what in Yiddish is called *tacheles*; or until the press conference after the meeting, when Varoufakis's newly won friends suddenly turn out to be old enemies, nothing personal of course; or when a secret appointment, secretively arranged by two might-be henchmen of a would-be big player at a far-off Berlin pizzeria, turns out to be anything but secret, watched from afar by one-cannot-exactly-know-who, certainly Mario from the ECB, perhaps Wolfgang, or even Angela?

Much is going on – is being performed – in this world, the pace is fast, new things pop up every day, opportunities beckon, losses must be dealt with. Varoufakis is to be admired for how he managed to reconstruct what happened in his half year of fame, or what appeared to be happening. In the end, however, nothing changed: in the eye of the storm, a frenzied standstill. As the financial waterboarding – Varoufakis's felicitous term for 'the institutions' threatening to cut off the money supply to Greek banks – went on, Mario, Christine, Pierre, Sigmar, Jean-Claude, Michel and Emmanuel expressed different degrees of compassion while trying to explain in so many patient words that the inevitable would always remain exactly this: inevitable. They could afford to be kind, because they knew that in the systemic mush in which they had made their home, you can do what you want, it will never affect the underlying concrete. 'Conversations' take place with the peculiar Anglo-American civility bred in American elite colleges and Goldman Sachs boardrooms, in English and on a first-name basis. That civility was easily extended even to a stranger like Varoufakis, who might well have ended up in a leading position at the ECB, the IMF, the OECD, the WTO or wherever, had he been prepared, like them, to pretend believing in the reasonableness of the unreasonable.

Not that our hero had no allies. But they were a strange bunch composed of fellow lefties such as James Galbraith and fallen-from-grace political addicts of, in part, questionable pedigree, such as Larry Summers, Jeffrey Sachs, and Norman, Baron Lamont of Lerwick, former chancellor of the exchequer. In the end even a good deal of Scotch with Larry in a Washington bar didn't do the trick. All those emails, references, telephone calls, nightly conversations and the memos that sprang from them – one wonders whether any of the principals ever read them. The outcome was clear from the beginning, the law had long been laid out, the riot act read, the sentence written. Varoufakis, in his desperate attempt to understand what was happening to him, guessed that the padded cell in which he found himself was a product of German precision engineering. Apparently he concluded this from Schäuble's dominance in the Eurogroup, where 'Wolfgang' (nobody in Germany outside of his family would dare call him by his first name) with his bad English and frank impoliteness must have appeared to him, initially in any case, like the Lord of the Rings in person.

Perhaps it was his rude manners that led Varoufakis to make a consequential misjudgement: to believe that Schäuble was planning to eject Greece from the monetary union because he was 'anti-European'. In fact, Schäuble, as it turned out, was willing to pay for an expensive golden handshake for Greece, in an effort to salvage his project of a 'Europe' small and homogenous enough to be governed from of a neo-liberalized French-German centre. Concessions yes, but only outside the EMU, not inside, so that his French friends could not ask to be spared as well. Sensing the tensions between Schäuble and Merkel, Varoufakis seems to have compounded his mistake by fantasizing Merkel as the pro-European antipode to the anti-European Schäuble. Actually, as he only found out when the game was over, her 'Europe' was, out of loyalty to the geostrategic interests of the United States, bigger and therefore more heterogeneous than Schäuble's, including not just Greece but, as a future prospect, many other countries on the European periphery, from Serbia via Albania to Ukraine. Golden handshakes *verboten*, that Europe had to be kept together, if necessary, by more brutal means: financial waterboarding was included *not* as an incentive to exit but as an instrument of rule. It was this misunderstanding, which t turned Merkel into something like Europe's Mother Earth, that was all too eagerly subscribed to by Tsipras and his entourage and in the end broke the back of Syriza.

But was, and is, the Economic and Monetary Union really a German dictatorship? At no point does Varoufakis consider the possibility that, more profoundly, it may be a dictatorship of past stupidities enshrined in a quasi-constitution designed to be forever unchangeable. Not a 'deep establishment' but a deep structure; an empire of errors as much as a German empire: sovereign states, all fiercely determined to remain exactly this, sharing a common currency without sharing sovereignty. Inexplicably the fundamental perversity of this construction entirely escaped Varoufakis, as evidenced in the recurrent moments when he demands respect for the national sovereignty of Greece, only to be told, by Schäuble of course, that under the EMU there is also German sovereignty, and Finnish sovereignty, and a lot more sovereignties. Where Varoufakis wants 'Europe' to honour the outcome of the Greek election, Schäuble tries in vain to make him understand that Germany has elections too, and a Constitutional Court to boot. This meant, in brutal simplicity, that no default could be allowed nor could debt be forgiven – only loans, meaning new debt, and only on condition of 'structural reforms', i.e., more austerity shrinking the economy and thereby increasing the debt further. Up to the present day, it seems that Varoufakis, unlike his Syriza friends-turned-traitors, has failed to comprehend that his demand for a clean break with 'Bailoutistan' and with the madness of 'expansionary contraction' was tantamount to an attack on the armoured institutional concrete underneath the political mush of 'Europe', an attack that could not but end in defeat.

As the 'players' Varoufakis encountered on their Brussels, Paris, Frankfurt and Berlin playgrounds tried, without effect, to convey to him, this did not mean that nothing could be done. Once the inevitabilities were understood, there were all sorts of palliatives and pain killers available from Dr Draghi's pharmacy, provided they could be administered in secret, so as to not wake up the unwashed. Help, yes, but only as long as the dirty secrets were not spilt. Since Varoufakis didn't or wouldn't get it, he eventually had to be sent off the pitch. Had he got it, Mario and Christine and Pierre and the others would undoubtedly have been more than happy to come up with ever new ingenious tricks, like creative state financing through the purchase of worthless loans from bankrupt banks. But *wer nicht hören will*, Schäuble can safely be assumed to have said, or mumbled, *muss fühlen*: he who refuses to see the world as it is shall suffer the consequences.

What is outright amazing to the attentive reader of Varoufakis is that whatever accidents happened to him on his journey through the European jungle of indolence and intrigue, he never lost his religious belief in 'Europe', 'European solidarity', 'European democracy', and generally 'the European project' – which he assumed as a matter of course to mean debt relief for Greece. In many ways this reminds one of those faithful functionaries of the Comintern in the 1920s and 1930s, who would not recognize the monster they were serving when it had already begun devouring them. At every turn in the way, even while being waterboarded by Wolfgang, Jeroen, Mario and friends, Varoufakis would protest that he was a deeply devoted 'Europeanist' whose one and only desire it was to keep Greece not only in the EU but also in the euro. Indeed, shortly after the system had finished with him,

Varoufakis founded and appointed himself leader of an organization called the Democracy in Europe Movement (DiEM25), of
which nothing has been heard for some time. One can be sure that,
listening to his Euro-enthusiastic confessions, the old boys and
girls inside the beast – the courtiers of Queen TINA – soon ceased
being afraid of this new kid on the block with his bizarre *amour
fou* for a Europe that did not and would never exist. If he really
meant what he said – and oddly enough he seemed to – he would
not be a problem: even if kicked out, he wouldn't rock the boat
because, for whatever reason, he had fallen in love with it.

How in the world could Varoufakis the accomplished academic
game theorist have hoped to extract concessions from the Empire
by assuring it of his everlasting allegiance? In part, perhaps, as a
reward for his true-blue eyes and for voluntarily and unilaterally
depriving himself, in proof of his European loyalty, of the possibility of entering the Brussels negotiating room with Grexit strapped
around his waist and addressing Wolfgang and company like this:
Look, if you don't listen I'll blow myself up right here by default-
ing on the Greek debt and exiting from the euro, and while I may
go under as a result, you know what? You and all your works will
go under with me. But rather than instilling the fear of the Lord in
his European enemies – as his despised domestic opponents within
Syriza, the Left Platform, had counselled – Varoufakis politely
asked for a consensual restructuring of the Greek public debt, on
the correct premise that the Greek state had already for some time
been bankrupt.

Correct premises, however, were not what Wolfgang was interested in. Quite simply, they were not what he had promised to his
parliamentary party, or what its members felt capable of selling to
their voters. What he could offer to Varoufakis was more of the
same: yet another loan in return for more austerity and 'structural
reforms', a loan that would mostly go not to Greece at all but
directly to Greece's creditors. Sign on the dotted line, Varoufakis
heard again and again, or else Mario will end the flow of euro cash

to Greek banks and Greek citizens, or threaten to do so and thereby cause a bank run that will finish off your puny government. So to extract from his new friends the debt relief, real and visible rather than under the counter, that he thought his country needed, Varoufakis the game theorist required a 'deterrent', ferocious enough that for using it he would need the firm support of his comrades at home. That deterrent was to be a unilateral restructuring of Greek government bonds purchased by the ECB from Greek banks under its Outright Monetary Transactions programme to inject 'liquidity' into the 'markets'. By unilaterally restructuring that debt, Varoufakis was certain, the Syriza government would force the German Constitutional Court to declare OMT illegal under German and European law, which in turn would force Mario to end it, which would eventually blow up the euro and the Eurozone – something like this. Varoufakis managed to get Tsipras and his 'war cabinet' to enter with him into what he calls a 'covenant', early on and then again and again as events unfolded, to the effect that Greece would actually use that deterrent if 'Europe' was to cause a shutdown of the Greek banking system, aware that such use would destroy what they had claimed was their beloved 'Europe' and its equally beloved currency.

With hindsight, even a child can see that this could have never worked, and Angela Merkel, whatever else she is, is not a child. You didn't have to be a genius Machiavellian to detect the weak spot in the Varoufakis scheme, and the reader remains mystified as to why it should have escaped Varoufakis that he was checkmated long before he made his first move. Blowing up what you hate may come easy to you. Before you blow up what you love you think twice. And it doesn't take much to make you think twice; just small concessions fed to you one by one, always at the last moment, giving you reason upon reason to postpone igniting the nuke. Little is needed to make one prefer life over death. And of course it doesn't hurt at all for your opponents to speak to those on whose support the man at the front ultimately depends. Tell them he is getting irrational, emotional, erratic, unpredictable – and the press will help with a concerted campaign of character assassination. So Merkel, queen of destructive ambiguity, unintelligible public speech and inscrutable public silence, designated by Varoufakis himself as the good cop to be turned to for help against Wolfgang the bad cop, opened a line to Tsipras to explain to him how the world really works and why his 'covenant' with Varoufakis was not mushy enough to be of use in the great mush of European politics. Perhaps she even pointed out that Varoufakis's deterrent had only ever existed in his imagination? Clearly Mario and the gang would have found ways to convince the German Constitutional Court and others practiced in euro-loyal Orwellianism that a Greek haircut on the bonds now held by the ECB, would it ever come to pass, was no haircut at all, and in any case could not be allowed to upset the ECB's commendable manoeuvres to save the greatest achievement of 'Europe', its common currency.

The high point of Varoufakis's story – one of several reasons why reading it is a must – is his final conversations with Wolfgang Schäuble, when the two suddenly became something like co-conspirators against their superiors, Merkel and Tsipras. Plain words were spoken, and we cannot escape a sense of tragedy as we observe Schäuble realizing, with astounding dignity, that his Franco-German dream of a lifetime was about to fall apart. 'You must tell [the Greek people] that if they want the euro they must have the MoU' – the latest version of the Memorandum of Understanding, the Troika's credit-for-austerity-plus-reform diktat. 'If they don't want the MoU, then that's fine, move on. Just move on'. A referendum, Schäuble suggests, would be the way out, and if it took six months or so to prepare, intermediate funding of the Greek state – which had been declared legally impossible by the assembled Troika – would be made available. Greeks, Schäuble was convinced, would see the light and exit – perhaps just for a while, 'with huge help from us,' until devaluation of a new drachma would have restored the country's economic competitiveness. 'The

MoU is bad for your people. It will not allow you to recover . . .'
And then, for the history books:

> 'In the Eurogroup you are probably the one who understands
> that the eurozone is unsustainable', [Schäuble] said. 'The euro-
> zone is constructed wrongly. We should have a political union,
> there is no doubt about it.'
>
> 'I always knew you to be a dedicated federalist', I inter-
> rupted . . . 'I am sure Mrs Merkel could not see as well as you
> did the importance of a federal political structure to go along
> with the monetary union.'
>
> He seemed pleased for a moment. 'And the French too', he
> added. 'They opposed me.'
>
> 'I know', I said. 'They wanted to use your Deutschmark but
> without sharing sovereignty.'
>
> Wolfgang agreed heartily. 'Yes, this is so. And I won't accept
> it. So, you see', he continued, 'the only way I can keep this thing
> together, is by greater discipline. Anyone who wants the euro
> must accept discipline. And it will be a much stronger eurozone
> if it is disciplined by Grexit.'

It is at this point that Varoufakis, his 'Europeanist' passions notwithstanding, decides to explore how 'huge' the 'help' would be
that Schäuble might arrange – which suggests that he had become
willing to reconsider his, until then, categoric rejection of Grexit.
While Tsipras allowed Varoufakis to seek further clarifications,
however, Merkel would not have any of this and apparently told
Schäuble so in no uncertain terms. On 8 June 2015, Schäuble and
Varoufakis talked for the last time, in Berlin at the German Finance
Ministry.

> Only a move beyond reasoning and rhetoric could break the
> vicious cycle, I thought, a human gesture. 'Will you do me
> favour, Wolfgang?' I asked humbly. He nodded warmly . . .

'I need to ask you to forget for a few minutes that we are ministers. I want to ask you for your advice . . . Will you do this for me?'

Under the watchful eyes of his deputies, he nodded again. Taking heart, I thanked him and sought his answer as an elder statesman, not an enforcer. 'Would you sign the MoU if you were in my place?' . . . [H]e looked out of the window. By Berlin standards, it was a hot and sunny day. Then he turned and stunned me with his answer. 'As a patriot, no. It's bad for your people . . .'

As I departed that day, I was not leaving behind me a Machiavellian dictator; I was leaving a sunken heart, a man ostensibly more powerful than almost anyone in Europe who nevertheless felt utterly powerless to do what he felt was right.

Probably Schäuble knew by then that Merkel was working hard with her new favourite disciple, Tsipras, to teach him how to govern Merkel-style – for example, let his people vote and then tell them they had voted for the opposite of what they had thought they were voting for. And indeed, the day after the Greek people had said no, Tsipras fired Varoufakis and said yes to another MoU even more ferocious than its predecessors, accompanied, however, by an extension of the Greek debt until never-ever day. Only a few weeks later, the opening of the German borders to a million refugees diverted public attention from the way Greece had once again been rescued by Germany and 'Europe'.

CHAPTER 7

The Politics of Depoliticization

July 2014

MUCH OF WHAT IS now mainstream political science tends to be rather boring. Following the lead of American departments and journals, research on issues of real intrinsic interest, such as the changing character of political parties, seems to be stuck in endless attempts to model the choice between office-seeking and policy-seeking, the interaction between 'vote-maximizing' parties and 'utility-maximizing' voters, the organization of voter preferences or the dynamics of coalition formation – all in timelessly general property spaces, designed to lend themselves to representation by complex sets of formal equations.

There are, however, exceptions. Among the most remarkable of these, until his untimely death in the summer of 2011, was Peter Mair, professor of comparative politics at the European University Institute in Florence. Widely respected, especially on the European side of his profession, Mair preserved a keen understanding of both the history and the purpose of the study of democracy. Unlike many in the field, he never lost sight of the close relationship between mass political parties and democratic outcomes; his work always considered the development of the former firmly in the context of the latter, as the more important of the two. Moreover, his concern was unabashedly with popular democracy and the enfranchisement of ordinary people, rather than with the abstract rules of decision-making that have become the favourite subject of much of what today passes as democratic theory.

Ruling the Void is the latest and, sadly, the last of Mair's books.* It completes an oeuvre that began with *The Changing Irish Party System* (1987), a still unsurpassed study of his native land, and continued with the landmark *Identity, Competition and Electoral Availability* (1990), co-authored with Stefano Bartolini, which focused on the striking long-term stability of Western party systems, albeit eroded by growing electoral volatility from the 1970s. This was followed by the elegant *Party System Change* (1997), and a series of collaborative collections. *Ruling the Void* was still unfinished when Mair passed away, although the core arguments were all in place. It is the merit of Francis Mulhern, a friend since student days, to have organized what there was into an immensely readable and coherent sequence, drawing on additional material to compose the long chapter on the European Union with which the book concludes. Mair's incisive style, in particular his ability to find clear and pointed formulations for what he had to say, is apparent from the opening lines:

> The age of party democracy has passed. Although the parties themselves remain, they have become so disconnected from the wider society, and pursue a form of competition that is so lacking in meaning, that they no longer seem capable of sustaining democracy in its present form.

In what follows, this premise is elaborated with the aid of an impressive array of empirical data, as Mair details the decline, from

---

* Peter Mair, *Ruling the Void: The Hollowing of Western Democracy*, London and New York: Verso, 2013.

below, of voter turnout and party memberships, and, from above, the 'withdrawal of the elites' from democratic accountability. Though we cannot know what *Ruling the Void* might have looked like had Mair had time to finish it, we can be confident that the grand outlines would have stayed the same, not least the author's steadfast refusal to retreat from the big questions in favour of methodological purity. Particularly striking is Mair's deep appreciation for political parties as intermediary agencies between their voters and the political institutions of the state – two realms with very different dynamics and strategic contingencies. It counts among Mair's great achievements as a political scientist that he resisted specializing in either one of these, though both require command of highly specific bodies of knowledge and research methodologies. For Mair, it was precisely their mediation between these two fields of action that defined the role of political parties; it was the way their responses in both zones were determined and combined that interested him most.

What, then, is the message of this important book? Going beyond the standard format of comparative politics, Mair looks less at national differences between party systems than at commonalities and shared historical trajectories. The 'golden age' of representative democracy is briefly sketched. With the advent of universal suffrage around the turn of the twentieth century, the earlier 'parties of notables' were supplanted by mass-membership organizations with strong, hierarchical structures, unifying voters on the basis of shared social experiences and collective hopes for what the party would achieve in government. The party's role was to translate its voters' interests into public policy, to recruit and promote political leaders capable of exercising executive power, and to compete for control of the executive through national elections. The classic mass party, Mair writes, 'gave voice to the people', while also ensuring that the institutions of government were accountable. Mair describes the development of mainstream parties from around the mid-1960s towards what the social democratic political scientist Otto Kirchheimer had described as a 'catch-all' model, seeking to scoop up votes far beyond their core constituencies and becoming 'primarily office-seeking parties, with the desire to occupy government winning priority over any sense of representational integrity'. The next stage, gathering steam from the mid-1980s and 1990s, is what Mair and Richard Katz, again following Kirchheimer, have called 'government by cartel', characterized by the elimination of effective opposition – the situation that prevails 'when no meaningful differences divide the party protagonists, however vigorously they may at times compete with one another'.

The last decades of the twentieth century thus witnessed 'a gradual but also inexorable withdrawal of the parties from the realm of civil society towards the realm of government and the state'. As Mair emphasizes, this 'withdrawal of the elites' has been paralleled by citizen disengagement, with steady falls in average turnout, decade by decade, and the 'passing of popular involvement' in political life. The process involved a downgrading of 'the party on the ground' in favour of 'the party in parliament', or in government, as leaders opted – to use another of Mair's memorable pairs of concepts – for 'responsibility' at the expense of 'responsiveness'. And while parties have drawn farther away from their voters, they have moved closer to each other: 'What remains is a governing class.'

Mair is careful to avoid monocausal narratives – or, indeed, any uni-directional causal reasoning. He attributes the 'hollowing out' of democratic party government to cumulative changes in the constraints and opportunities parties confront in the realms between which they have traditionally mediated: their social bases, on the one hand, and the pay-off matrices of the political arena, on the other. These involve two general trends: individualization and globalization. The first refers to the erosion of the cohesive social environments that helped structure the original growth of mass parties – the world of trade unions, clubs, churches, business associations, farming groups, and so on – as well as the fragmentation of collective identities, including that of the industrial working class. Individualization in its various expressions is invoked to explain an increasing indifference and apathy among citizens with respect to collective interests and politics, amounting to a secular disintegration of the modern 'demos'.

Globalization, meanwhile, stands for the declining ability of national governments to shape autonomous policies. The two trends have a similar effect on party government. 'Whether circumscribed by global or European constraints, or limited by their inability to identify a sufficiently large and cohesive constituency to offer a mandate for action', Mair writes, 'parties increasingly tend to echo one another and to blur what would otherwise be clear policy choices'. Moreover, faced with an eroding social base, party elites have sought refuge in the security offered by state institutions to politicians willing to agree to a 'sharing of office, programme and voters'. In the process, political decision-making has migrated to 'non-majoritarian' (that is, elite) institutions, like central banks and regulatory agencies, which are insulated from 'majoritarian' redistributive pressures – pressures to which governments would in any case struggle to respond, once globalization had undermined the economic powers of nation-states, formerly the seats of popular democracy.

Mair's Exhibit A of a political system of depoliticized expert 'governance', specifically constructed to exclude parties, popular democracy and, with them, redistributive politics, is, of course, the European Union, as analysed in the book's final chapter. It is testimony to Mair's sharp analytical mind that he understood the political-economic logic of this entity so much better than the hosts of political scientists specializing in the study, not to say the celebration, of 'European integration', whose main achievement has been to discover a 'democratic deficit' in a political system in which the protection of collective decision-making from democracy was nothing less than the founding principle. The chapter leaves no illusions as to the possibility, tirelessly conjured up by the 'democratization' rhetoric of the 'more Europe' forces, of recasting the EU as a base of resistance against the disempowering effects of capitalist internationalization. As Mair points out, referencing Robert Dahl's reflections on opposition, 'we are afforded the right to be represented in Europe, even if it is sometimes difficult to work out when and how this representative link functions; but we are not afforded the right to organize opposition within the European polity':

> We know that a failure to allow for opposition within the polity is likely to lead either (a) to the elimination of meaningful opposition, and to more or less total submission, or (b) to the mobilization of an opposition of principle against the polity – to anti-European opposition and to Euroscepticism. And indeed, this development is also reaching down into the domestic sphere, where the growing weight of the EU, and its indirect impact on national politics, also helps to foster democratic deficits, and hence also limits the scope for classical opposition at the national level.

Mair concludes on a note of lucid reflection: by losing opposition, we lose voice, and by losing voice, we lose control of our own political systems; it is not at all clear how that control might be regained, he writes, and meaning restored to that 'great milestone' of democracy – opposition.

Ruling the Void is essential reading for anyone concerned with twenty-first-century politics. Compelling as it is, however, there are a number of intriguing issues on which the book remains ambiguous. One is *why* mainstream political parties in the West severed ties to their social bases and adopted the neoliberal *pensée unique* from the 1980s onwards. Was it because changed objective conditions left them no choice, was it organizational opportunism – the attractions of technocratic power-sharing – or

was it because their constituents had deserted them and were no
longer available for collective mobilization? At one point, Mair
states unequivocally that the withdrawal was mutual – 'this is the
conclusion that needs to be most clearly underlined'; but he does
not explore the precise nature of this mutuality. Nor does he
discuss the more general issue of whether there might be a relationship of causation between the two trends, or in which direction
that might operate; whether each retreat has depended on the
other, and how far they have been mutually reinforcing.

It is here, in particular, that one most wishes Mair could have
had the time to respond to a number of questions that might have
pushed his analysis further. One concerns his key concept of
globalization and what it stands for. That the growing internationalization of the capitalist economy from the 1980s onwards has
made it more difficult for national governments to intervene on
behalf of popular majorities is widely known. But pressures for the
protection of capital accumulation against democratic interfer-
ence are older than that; they suggest a deeper tension between
capitalism and democracy which was only provisionally suspended
during the few decades of post-war growth. Remaining on his
home turf of political science, Mair refrains from venturing
into political economy, even though the trends he describes – the
transfer of economic policy to 'non-accountable', technocratic
institutions; the elimination of egalitarian redistribution from
Western governments' political agendas – suggest the rise of a
new political-economic regime, after the victory of capital in the
struggles of the 1970s.

Mair's story about the hollowing of mass democracy would fit
nicely with a more general account of the transformation of the
post-war Keynesian growth regime – which was obliged to look
for economic progress through redistribution from the top to the
bottom – into a Hayekian one, which puts its hope in redistribution from the bottom to the top. More generally, it could be
placed in the context of a basic dilemma for democratic politics

under capitalism: the fact that egalitarian democracy may, in good times, help to manage the social tensions produced by the nature of the capitalist accumulation process, yet in the process may cause economic turmoil – capital flight and so on – that undermines the preconditions of successful government. In a situation like this, governing parties may feel they have little choice but to become 'responsible' and make their peace with the capitalist class, while protecting themselves as best they can from pressures to be 'responsive' to their members and voters.

Another question is whether the major political parties would actually stand a chance today of organizing and mobilizing their constituents in ways that were taken for granted in the 1970s. Mair emphasizes the individualization and fragmentation of their social bases, which had become a general phenomenon by the 1990s, and which weakened parties of the Left in particular. But this may be just the surface of a more profound change in the way people relate to each other, indeed in the very nature of sociability and social structure – a change we may only now begin to understand, with the breakthrough of so-called social media. Individualization, as invoked by Mair and others, seems to be no more than a provisional concept for an increasing short-termism and volatility affecting social commitments in general, not just in civic and political, but also in private and family life, and certainly in labour and product markets; a trend portrayed by many as a gain in freedom rather than a loss of solidarity. What this augurs for politics may perhaps include 'voice', in Albert Hirschman's sense, but primarily 'exit', early and often, and very little 'loyalty' when it comes to the compromise and discipline in the service of shared values necessary for a collective vision of the good society.

In the order that seems to be emerging, social bonds are construed as a matter of taste and choice rather than of obligation, making communities appear as voluntary associations from which one can resign if they require excessive self-denial, rather than as 'communities of fate' with which one either rises or goes under. The new social media that have fast become almost indispensable tools of human sociability enable people to connect and associate with like-minded others on the most esoteric 'subjective' matters. As cyberspace trumps geography, the connection, elementary for traditional political mobilization, is broken between shared interests and personal relations arising from physical vicinity. One consequence is that social control among 'network members' is minimized; dropping out is easy, especially when people use pseudonyms – another facet of the new voluntarism of social relationships. Browsing the boundless supply of causes, tastes and lifestyles made available by the internet, one can freely decide to 'like' whatever one wishes; in contrast to old-school political parties, there is no pressure for ideological consistency or for adherence to a common programme.

The analogy between the consumerization of political commitment and the new markets of hedonistic lifestyle capitalism, fed by individually customized products, is hard to overlook. Thus, as part of a national effort to boost voter turnout in the May 2014 European Parliament elections, the *Frankfurter Allgemeine* offered its readers an online quiz – put together, incidentally, by the European University Institute in Florence – under the title 'Which party best fits me?', rather than, as one might naively have expected, 'Which party best fits Europe?' Meanwhile, all critical issues of European policy had been carefully sidelined by the two old Brussels hands who presented themselves as continental Spitzenkandidaten for the presidency of the European Commission. While pretending to compete with each other, they ran on essentially identical platforms. No better confirmation can be found for Mair's theses on 'government by cartel' and the brilliant analysis of EU politics offered in the final chapter of *Ruling the Void*.

Mair offers two explanations, as noted earlier, for his finding that mainstream political parties have withdrawn from their intermediary position between their constituents and the state. One is that objective political-economic circumstances have made it impossible for them to remain responsive to popular needs and demands by binding them to policies unsuited to eliciting political and civic commitment. Second, he suggests that their social bases may no longer be amenable to the kind of collective action that parties traditionally inspired. If in the nineteenth century it was the *Lumpenproletariat* that was incapable of disciplined organization, today it may be the hedonistic middle class. An example of the desperate lengths to which the establishment parties now go to arrest the meltdown of their memberships would be the youth organization of the German CDU, which has launched a recruitment drive promoting the party colour, black – clerical in origin, deriving from the black frocks of Catholic priests – under the slogan, 'Black is beautiful'; in English, of course. CDU activists throw parties at which they distribute, among other things, black condoms.

What Mair fails to discuss, however, is whether these two trends, macro and micro, are in some way related. Several linkages could be contemplated, from the globalization of production systems and labour markets, eroding the class structures of advanced-capitalist societies, to the rise of consumer capitalism with its commercial individualization and privatization of need satisfaction.* The disturbing conclusion may be that in today's capitalism, systemic legitimacy derives from individualized consumption in markets unlimited by jurisdictional borders, rather than from the political correction of markets within the framework of nation-states or from democratic deliberation about collective interests in political communities. As individual consumer choice takes the place of political choice, the intermediation of interests by political organizations may come to be perceived as dispensable or, worse, constraining. Capitalist development may

---

* See 'Citizens as Customers: Considerations on the New Politics of Consumption', *New Left Review*, no. 76, July/August 2012, pp. 27–47.

have come to an important extent, and indeed more than ever, to consist of market *Vergesellschaftung* overwhelming and superseding political *Vergemeinschaftung*.

Mair's account focuses mainly on Western Europe and the new democracies in the East, to the neglect of the United States. There, the trend appears to be the opposite: growing polarization between the main political parties, declining willingness to compromise resulting in a general roadblock in government, a return to 'responsiveness' at the price of 'responsibility', with policy triumphing over office-seeking – all in contradiction to the established model of median voter dominance, as Jacob Hacker and Paul Pierson, authors of *Winner-Take-All Politics*, point out in a recent paper; all the more so, as voter preferences in the United States seem to have remained largely unchanged. The rebirth of ideological purity in the United States has taken place mainly on the Right, in the Republican Party, with Democrats basically remaining in a centrist position, which further deepens the divide between the two parties – hence the term 'asymmetric polarization'.

But why should one party in effect prevent itself from building a national majority, for the sake of more authentically representing a narrow core constituency? It is here that interest groups come in, especially those of capital – a subject Mair only marginally touches upon. In Hacker and Pierson's account, the American business lobby serves as a sort of functional equivalent to the European state, providing its preferred party with financial support, thus liberating it from servitude to the median voter. In a constitutional system of divided government, the party can then dedicate itself to blocking legislation, thereby preserving the institutional status quo in a world of rapid social and economic change. The result is what Hacker has elsewhere called policy 'drift': the gradual undermining of redistributive policies and institutions by denying them the regular update they require to keep pace with their changing environment. Neutralizing the state in this way can apparently be an effective political equivalent to 'globalization', in a country still hegemonic enough in principle to command realistic alternatives to neoliberalism.

How ironic that today re-politicization seems mainly confined to the Right, and not just in the United States; consider the new 'populist' parties in Europe that are in large part benefiting from the centre-left's abandonment of its old constituency, in pursuit of grand coalitions with the centre-right. As to organized interests, it is worth noting that, at the very time when 'catch-all' parties and their elites are engaged in an accelerated withdrawal from their social base, business associations in Europe have grown more attentive to their 'logic of membership', breaking free from corporatist entanglements with trade unions and the state and radicalizing their rhetoric, together with their political stance. These dynamics will only intensify the developments so finely etched in *Ruling the Void*.

CHAPTER 8

The Magic Word to End All Confusion

March 2015

THERE IS NO SHORTAGE of concepts of democracy, but with goodwill they can be divided into two groups: democracy as problem-solving, and democracy as redistribution. On the first view, democracy is a matter of efficiency and competence and concerns the problems of society as a whole. It is needed because it is more 'intelligent' (Carl Lindblom) and prevents 'pathological learning' in the centres of decision-making (Karl Deutsch): a good democracy is the best technocracy. On the other view, democracy is more about justice – or what the demos thinks justice is: the defence of ordinary people against the rich and powerful. Democracy of the second kind brings problems to the fore that usually languish in the background; it makes it harder to transform public into private power; it is not always intelligent, but poses a permanent threat to society's boardrooms; it is plebeian (or 'populist' according to today's usage) instead of academic; grubby like life itself, and a constant warning to bosses of all kinds not to regard their own interests as the interests of everyone else.

Helmut Willke, professor of global governance at Zeppelin University in Baden-Württemberg, leaves us in no doubt that his democracy belongs in the first group.* His world is the world of the 'knowledge society', not the trade union meeting. His democracy is about steering, not striking. Not a single word about power and counter-power, capital and labour, oligarchy and precariat; instead we hear a lot about intelligence and stupidity. That one person's problem might be another's solution doesn't feature. Even so, not all is well with democracy today; there are delays in the solving of problems resulting from 'confusion', generally because of ignorance and specifically because of 'globalization' and its consequences: increased interdependence between national and international 'problem-solving', between nation-states supposed to contribute to the production of global collective goods, and between problem areas whose complex interactions result in ever more unpredictable systemic risks.

Democracy, according to Willke, must improve if it is going to be equal to its rivals. These are three in number: Chinese dictatorship, the American finance-and-faith community, and European market-liberal technocracy. Reform Willke-style means improving the intelligence of democracy through better utilization of the expertise of the knowledge society. His model is the participation of civil-society organizations in the specialized institutions of global governance, such as the WTO, that have emerged out of the nation-state and are therefore immune to stupidity from below. Justice, defined as equalization of unequal life chances and political influence, would presumably ensue as a by-product of taking proper account of 'the facts'. The 'confusion of democracy' should be eliminated by a further confusion, this time a beneficial one, in the shape of an 'intelligent combination' of democratic and specialist decision-making. More precision seems to require heavy doses of globalist-technocratic poli-sci jargon, in English so as to be maximally opaque to German-reading know-nothings: what is

---

* Helmut Willke, *Demokratie in Zeiten der Konfusion* [Democracy in an Age of Confusion], Berlin: Suhrkamp, 2014.

to be aimed for is *smart governance, good governance, political restraint, best practice, communities of practice* and the empowerment of *epistemic communities,* producing *global law without a state,* with *zero trauma* and without *quick wins,* while sidelining the *median voter* and the *median official* that represents her.

Smart governance does provide for participation. It is, however, 'focused' and 'differentiated according to criteria of commitment, competence, degree of concern and sustainability based on professional expertise'. There is, Willke admits, an inevitable 'loss of formal democracy' of the 'one person, one vote' kind. But this is compensated for by 'material decision-making competence' – 'decision makers know what they are doing' – taking the place of the 'pervasive and inevitable ignorance of most people'. 'Ignorance', according to Willke, 'leads to exclusion. This exclusion is democratic because it affects the majority. The consequence is a mutual, many-layered dependence of experts on a multiplicity of other experts for an abundance of other questions and problems'.

As always when governance becomes an issue, difficulties arise about the role of the state. Allegedly it lacks *Kompetenzkompetenz*: the competence to allocate competencies. But, as a 'core competence', it still has a *Rahmenkompetenz* – a framework competence – which it may use for 'context-steering' and 'moderating subsystem discourses'. Even so, in Willke's view, 'the primacy of politics over capitalism' still holds good and 'democracy has it in its power to control and regulate capitalism so that it remains compatible with the fundamental principles of democracy', even if 'in practice . . . this is of course never guaranteed'. Hope dies last, and there's no harm in hoping anyway. In concrete terms, Willke appears to envisage a constitution in which parliament takes a back seat, delegating cognitively demanding questions to bodies of experts organized into theme-specific quasi-parliaments, 'carefully selected [by whom?] for their competence and the extent to which they are affected'. These will then take decisions that pay heed to vertical and horizontal interdependencies, including of course international ones, and to strategic goals and global interests that transcend legislative periods.

But who are the knowledge-society know-it-alls, the 'policy networks' whom democracy and the state are to endow with the power of governance? Willke's showcase example of independent regulators immune to populism and supported by specialist expertise compensating for the cognitive overload of the ordinary man and woman turns out to involve the very same central banks whose catastrophic failure in advance of 2008 is still fresh in our memories. Apart from the central banks, we are reduced to guesswork. Should the military community take over arms procurement? Should the banking association take over banking regulation? Should cyclists, sports physicians and pharmaceutical companies take over doping controls? Should goats be put in charge of the vegetable patches? Or should consumer associations be allowed to take part, as well as trades unions, the churches and the universities? And if so, why is this supposed to be smarter than democracy as we know it or, for that matter, the comitology of the European Union?

Willke's defence of democracy as problem-solving at the expense of democracy as redistribution must invite the question whether it doesn't throw the baby out with the bath water. As a systems theorist, Willke seems to believe that he has to write around a systems-theoretical problem that his teacher Luhmann, following Max Weber, formulated in a way that made it impossible to solve – probably with the precise intention to allow them to declare all solutions on offer systematically inadequate. For if it is true that the subsystems at work in modern societies (including the political one) function in a self-referential and 'operationally closed' manner, so that they can neither be controlled nor be used to control other systems from the outside, then it is not easy, to put it mildly, to conceive of a theory of governance as a systems-theoretical update of a theory of democracy. At any rate, reading Willke's book prompts the thought that without abandoning its premises, even the best-intentioned efforts to steer around the consequences of Luhmann-Weberian democratic-steering nihilism cannot produce anything better than true-blue hopes for constitutional amendments of a sort that everybody knows will never happen.

Perhaps a little less systems theory and some more of the good old theories of class, interest and power would have been helpful? A little more about politics and less about policies? It ought surely to be possible to ask whether the blame for the financial crisis really lies with a lack of knowledge, rather than with a politics which, under financialized capitalism, has become too dependent upon novel methods of 'surplus-making' (Marx) outside the 'real economy'. And is our lack of protection from global crises really due to formal problems of cooperation between fundamentally well-intentioned nation-states that are, unfortunately, caught up in 'confused' democratic institutions that give too much access to popular stupidity? According to Willke, 'At its core we need to make the transition from Pareto-optimal (negative) coordination to Kaldor-optimal (positive) coordination.' What could be easier than that, thinks the systems theorist? Would it not be better, answers the political economist, to begin with the imbalances of power and conflicts of interest, global and domestic, that rule our world, and not least with the decaying domestic politics of the declining capitalist hegemon, the United States, and its irresponsible deployment of the remnants of its hegemony in defence of its destructive self-interest?

CHAPTER 9

Neither Forwards nor Sideways. Perhaps Back?

March 2017

W HAT TO DO WHEN you're stuck – when you can go neither forwards nor backwards? Johannes Becker and Clemens Fuest advocate moving sideways.* The monetary union is a disaster, but the political union that might heal it will not happen, and we are not allowed to wish for a return to national currencies. Their 'pragmatic proposal' is for more national autonomy through less international dependency; more national democracy with more national responsibility; less politics and more technocracy on a European level, in exchange for less technocracy and more politics on the national level.

Why not move forward into the political union that should have preceded the monetary union? Braving possible denunciations as 'anti-European', Becker and Fuest explain to their readers that a European political union cannot emerge by bypassing the national states but only by working through them and on their foundations. This, however, comes up against insuperable conflicts

---

* Johannes Becker and Clemens Fuest, *Der Odysseus-Komplex: Ein pragmatischer Vorschlag zur Lösung der Eurokrise* [The Odysseus Complex: A Pragmatic Proposal to Resolve the Euro Crisis], Munich: Hanser, 2017.

between interests and ideas, particularly in what Germans like to refer to as 'core Europe': Germany and France. For Germany, a politically united Europe is one into which the member states dissolve, one way or other; for France, it is one in which France, in league with the Mediterranean countries, can outvote Germany. Neither project can win out over the other. A European system of public finance that could be ratified in France could not be ratified in Germany and vice versa.

Becker and Fuest trace the prehistory and the course of the European crisis back to its essentials, reconstructing it as a history of conflict between France and Germany, set in motion by Kohl and Mitterrand, continued by Schröder and Chirac, and reaching maturity under Merkel and Sarkozy and Merkel and Hollande. The theme is always Maastricht versus solidarity, adherence to rules versus further development of rules, do-it-yourself versus one-for-all-and-all-for-one. France hopes for resources and decisions to be transferred to the community, whereas Germany points to the Treaty of Maastricht, to be strictly adhered to as long as a political union doesn't yet exist – a union that, of course, could only ever be a decentralized federal state with a German political culture of stability and export-driven growth, not a European extension of the French model of statehood with politically controlled money and state-driven growth.

So what should be done, in a pragmatic step sideways towards 'resolving the euro crisis'? Becker and Fuest describe how ingenious new ways are constantly being sought and found in the European Council to introduce joint liability for the old and new debts of banks and states. Germany always gives way because, according to the authors, it has no concept of its own with which to oppose that of the French and their allies, namely solidarity, sovereignty and majority. Becker and Fuest omit the full list of the transgressions of Germany under Merkel, 'the planless hegemon', having relegated it to a newspaper article that appeared months before the book. On the other hand, they could not resist referring in the most politically incorrect terms to 8 May 2010, the day of the Brussels summit when Merkel allegedly fell into Sarkozy's trap, as the 'day of capitulation' – the capitulation of Germany, sixty-five years after 8 May 1945, as the self-certified representative of economic common sense.

Becker and Fuest make no secret of the fact that their 'pragmatic proposal' would open up an exceptionalist route for Germany to escape from the solidarity embrace of the Mediterranean nations. It would spell the end of Draghi's claim that 'the euro crisis is a history of things that Germany "will never accept" but ends up agreeing to', and Varoufakis's assertion that 'whatever the Germans say, they always end up paying'. This explains the book's leitmotif of the ingenious Odysseus, who ordered his crew to bind him to the mast of his ship so as to prevent him from being lured to a watery death by the song of the Sirens. Economists love this ancient story because they see it as proof that through rationally motivated self-restraint, and with the aid of appropriately constructed institutions, you can prevent yourself from acting irrationally against your own interests, when the flesh becomes too weak or outside pressures too powerful. The person to be strapped to the mast of reason is none other than Angela Merkel, who, the authors believe, has to be regularly rescued from the siren songs of Sarkozy, Hollande, Renzi, Draghi *e tutti quanti* – an idea that looks as though it came directly out of the house of Schäuble.

The proposals themselves that are supposed to put an end to the euro crisis appear less persuasive than their derivation. Crisis-prone spots to be repaired include the European Council and the European Central Bank. Their powers, mindlessly conceded by a succession of German political leaders, need to be radically curtailed in favour of the member states (who in return need to take responsibility for the effects of their policies on capital markets), and of new but now genuinely independent and tightly mandated technocratic authorities. 'All essential operative decisions' should be 'removed from the nocturnal negotiating sessions in Brussels' and either transferred to the member states or 'European technocratic institutions' with precisely defined 'guidelines' that are to be neither negotiable nor open to interpretation. Five procedural changes are to do the trick: banking regulation must be centralized and depoliticized, new government debt should be taken out only at a state's own risk and own interest rates; states should only be bailed out by means of automatic mechanisms agreed in advance and in line with unalterable decisions made 'on stock'. In addition, there should be debt conferences to restore access to the capital markets for over-indebted countries in crisis, and the remit of the ECB should be cut down to monetary policy in a narrow sense.

Becker and Fuest are aware that because their recipe for reform returns responsibility to the member states, it presupposes a 'demythologization' of the currency union (the present reviewer would prefer to call it a 'desacralization'): the realization that the latter is neither 'Europe' nor 'the European idea', but a currency regime, and a pretty misconceived one at that. The authors go so far as to refuse to consider the exit of individual countries to be a pan-European catastrophe, as any patriotic German is supposed to do. All this is accompanied by somewhat long-winded disquisitions to the effect that the reforms demanded by the authors would not only put an end to democratically dubious redistributions from country to country and from taxpayers to banks, but also that they constitute the last word in theoretical economic wisdom. At this point, there are some quite fierce outbursts against American fellow-economists – unusual, to put it mildly, from their normally deeply deferential German disciples – in particular, to the extent that they adhere to neo-Keynesian ideas on fiscal and monetary expansion. Who is in the right is less interesting than the fact that the relevant passages read like speaking notes for the Federal finance minister in the face of a collapse of the EMU at some future Eurogroup meeting.

In any case, it is hard to imagine that the authors really believe that their 'pragmatic proposal' could become reality. France and Co., if they act according to the account of them given in the book, are unlikely, to say the least, to help Germany immunize itself against political pressure. (Not even the ingenious Odysseus would have come up with the idea of asking the Sirens to help tie him to the mast.) True enough, they propose, almost as an aside, to buy the agreement of Germany's partners by taking over their outstanding liabilities. But how to get this past the European Council and the Bundestag they never ask or explain, just as they avoid the question of why the new rules introduced in exchange for Germany providing debt relief for Europe should not, in the next crisis, be subject to the same interpretative and revisionist pressures as the Maastricht rules today.

In fact the situation is even more complicated. If Merkel always relents, it is because German export industries, if not already dear to her heart then heavily on her back, do not care in the least how much German taxpayers have to pay for the euro. But will they forever be willing to pay German exporters' entrance fee to their captive Eurozone markets? Whereas Becker and Fuest's Odysseus problem – and why that problem has become a 'complex' in their book title, as with Oedipus, is something that the publisher's marketing department may be able to explain – consists in protecting the German government from agreeing to foot the bill, the German government's problem is that footing that bill is becoming increasingly risky if it wishes to survive politically. Even a red-green-red government (of the SPD, the Greens, and the Linkspartei) would discover that as far as Europe is concerned, the era of 'permissive consensus' lies irrevocably in the past. For that reason too, 'pragmatic' reforms à la Odysseus may no longer be needed: political blood is thicker than institutional water. Obviously this will do nothing to end the European crisis but will instead intensify it, given that the expectations of other European states with respect to German behaviour date from the Kohl and

Merkel eras with their silver-plated 'commitment' to the 'European idea'. The enduring gap between what has come to be expected from the past and what will be possible in the future, easily attributable to the ill will or the stupid irrationality of Swabian housewives of every political hue, is likely to give rise to a deep, lasting conflict that may well tear 'Europe' apart.

If 'sideways' is not an option, then, might it be worth trying to move backwards after all? It is striking that the only arguments Becker and Fuest advance against a solution through dissolution come right out of the very inventory of Euro-pious articles of faith that they have otherwise so refreshingly forsworn. At their core is France and the fears that an end to the euro might provoke there. But this overlooks the fact that there are now two different schools of thought in France. On the one hand, there is the centrist view on both the Right and the Left that the currency union is needed to 'bind' Germany into France's European sphere of interest. On the other hand, there are those on both sides who have given up on the euro because they think that it doesn't bind Germany to France but, instead, France to Germany. Also overlooked is Italy, where the wish to be free from the euro already has majority support, not least because of disappointment that the German compensation they have been promised by the French is unlikely ever to arrive. Can it be the case that by presenting an evidently unrealizable solution as 'pragmatic', and simultaneously advancing such thin arguments against a nonpragmatic dissolution, Becker and Fuest tacitly aim to bring their readers to the point of exploring dispassionately once again a way out that all right-thinking people are expected to consider impossible?

CHAPTER 10

Scenario for a Wonderful Tomorrow

March 2016

EUROPE – MORE PRECISELY, *EUROPA,* or *l'Europe Bruxelloise* – is falling apart, blown up *aus Versehen* by its most devoted fans, the Germans. In the summer of 2015, having humiliated the Greeks by forcing another reform diktat down their throats, Angela Merkel started a new game, diverting attention from the economic and political disaster monetary union had become. Abrupt changes of policy are nothing new to Merkel, who is best described as a postmodern politician with a Machiavellian disdain for both causes and people. Having made her party adopt a radically neoliberal, deregulationist anti-labour platform in 2003, she barely escaped defeat two years later at the hands of Gerhard Schröder, who had long lost his capacity to govern. When she became chancellor, she used her office and the Grand Coalition with the post-Schröder Social Democratic Party (SPD) to purge her party of neoliberalism and neoliberals, and social-democratize it beyond recognition. In 2011, after the nuclear accident at Fukushima, which received extensive media coverage in Germany, it took Merkel, then known as *Atomkanzlerin,* no more than a few days to order the immediate closure of eight nuclear power plants and to initiate legislation to end all nuclear power generation by 2022 at the latest. This was only a few months after she had, with much political arm-twisting, got the Bundestag to repeal the nuclear phase-out passed by the Red-Green coalition in 2001, and to extend the operating licenses of German nuclear plants by an average of ten years.

In 2015 the refugee crisis offered Merkel another opportunity to demonstrate how fast she can change tack. Once again, media coverage influenced her decision-making, just as it would a few months later when smartphone videos of the New Year's Eve riot at Cologne Central Station triggered another 180 degree turn. In July a PR event, part of a government campaign in which cabinet members met ordinary citizens to listen to their ideas of the 'good life', went wrong. One of the young people invited to take part in a 'dialogue' with Merkel on the environment, the fourteen-year-old daughter of Palestinian asylum seekers, unexpectedly complained in front of the TV cameras that her family, who had been living in Germany for four years, might be sent back to the Lebanon at any moment. She asked, in flawless German, why she wasn't allowed to stay in Germany 'to enjoy life like everybody else'. Merkel said something like, 'We cannot take in everyone, much as we might want to.' The girl began to cry. Not knowing what to do, Merkel started patting her head with a helpless expression on her face. The result was widespread outrage on social media, a world that Merkel's aides watch and analyse at least as carefully as they do what goes on inside her party. A few months later, the authorities told the girl's family that they could stay in Germany for at least another year.

As reports on the suffering migrants at several European borders filled the news, the German political class became persuaded that the German public would never put up with images like those of the Jungle in Calais. Day after day the media, whipped into a frenzy by Facebook and Twitter, accused France and Britain of callously denying migrants' human rights. Then, in September, the publication of the photograph of the dead Syrian child, Alan

Kurdi, who had drowned together with his mother and five-year-old brother attempting to cross the sea into Greece, forced political leaders worldwide into hectic if symbolic activity. Among Germans it was widely believed that the boy's death was the fault of 'Europe' as a whole, including Germany, the country that the boy's family had been trying to reach. Meanwhile, refugees had been gathering in increasing numbers at Budapest's central station, which produced another set of powerful images; most of them indicated that they were heading for Germany.

If a master politician like Merkel has any fixed principle, it is never to let a good crisis go to waste. It wasn't just media stories about suffering migrants that led her to invite the refugees in Budapest to come to Germany, no papers required and no questions asked. What Merkel called 'showing a friendly face in an emergency' was apt to shame those who, during the euro crisis, had enjoyed the cartoons of Merkel and her finance minister, Wolfgang Schäuble, in Nazi uniforms. By opening its borders while the French and British borders remained closed, the German government could hope to recapture the moral high ground occupied for so long by those accusing it of pitiless sado-monetarism, or worse.

Another factor was the tight labour market that German employers, still Merkel's main constituency, were facing, especially after the introduction of a statutory minimum wage was forced on Merkel by her coalition partner, the SPD. For a while, enthusiasm had run high about the arrival of university-trained Spanish engineers, driven by the crisis in their own country to take up employment in German automobile factories.* But freedom-of-movement immigration from inside the EU was not enough to close the German demographic gap or secure the

---

*   Germany is today the prosperity region of the Economic and Monetary Union, which may be seen as an integrated transnational economy characterized by rapidly increasing regional disparities. Germany relates to Spain as Baden-Württemberg to Mecklenburg-Vorpommern, or Lombardy to Sicily.

long-term solvency of the German social security system. A consulting firm working for the Federal government, Prognos, estimated in 2016 that Germany would need 500,000 immigrants per year for the next fifteen years if the country was to avoid a decline in labour supply. Rumours spread in the German press that among Syrian refugees in particular, many would bring along degrees in engineering and medicine, or all manner of other skills. German economic research institutes predicted a new wave of economic growth, while employers promised to invest heavily in training the presumably tiny number of less skilled immigrants. Everybody assumed that most if not all of the refugees and asylum seekers – a distinction soon lost in the general excitement – would be staying in Germany for a long time if not for good.

For Merkel, who in October 2010 had claimed that 'the *multikulti* approach [had] failed, absolutely failed', this was no longer a problem. In fact, it had become a solution: in the first half of 2015 several studies indicated that the expensive policy measures taken over a decade of Merkel rule to induce German families to have more children had had next to no effect. Early that summer, to avert what was perceived as a looming demographic crisis, Merkel got her closest aides to test the mood in the party and among the general public on immigration legislation, but was met with firm resistance. The result must have been a strong temptation to use refugee and asylum policy as a substitute for immigration policy proper – as immigration policy by the back door.* Unlike conventional immigration, responsibility for which would have had to be accepted by the government, immigration by asylum could be presented as a humanitarian obligation, and indeed one enshrined in international law, to which there was 'no alternative'.

---

* See David Abraham, 'The Refugee Crisis and Germany: From Migration Crisis to Immigration and Integration Regime', University of Miami Legal Studies Research Paper nos. 16–17, 1 February 2016.

Budapest was what the ancient Greeks called a *kairos* – a lucky moment when a number of birds were positioned in such a way that they could be killed with one stone. Politics, as always with Merkel, trumped policies. 'Showing a friendly face' would make it possible for the Greens in 2017 to do what their leadership has long wanted but never dared: form a coalition government with the Christian Democrats. Merkel acted exactly as she had on neoliberal reform in 2005 and on nuclear energy in 2011: quickly, on her own, and without wasting time explaining herself. Just as when she ordered the *Energiewende* [energy transition] while her legislation extending the operation of the nuclear power plants was still on the books (several energy supply companies are suing for damages), she counted on the Bundestag opposition – the Linkspartei and the Greens – not to ask awkward questions, and they obliged. The members of her own party couldn't complain: they had been backed into a corner by the SPD's approval of Merkel's stance, and by their desire not to damage their leader. Once again, a decision 'that will change our country', as Merkel herself put it, was made without regard for democratic process or, for that matter, constitutional formalities. When Merkel declared the German borders open, there had been no cabinet decision to this effect and no government statement in the Bundestag. Since the opposition never inquired, as Merkel knew they wouldn't, nobody knows to this day what sort of order, legal or not, by whom and when, was given to the police. The Interior Ministry is still refusing requests from leading figures in German public law (including the former president of the Constitutional Court, who was preparing a legal opinion on the matter for the Bavarian government) for access to the ministerial decree that should have been issued to the border authorities.*

---

* According to investigative journalist Robin Alexander, the government originally intended to open the border for just one weekend to allow the migrants at Budapest Central Station to cross through Austria and reach Germany, and an order to close it again

There were, one should think, good reasons for asking questions. The refugees, more than a million of them, who arrived in Germany in 2015, all arrived from safe third countries. Under German and European law, they had to register in the country where they first entered the European Union, and then wait to be assigned a legal residence in a member state. The German government seems to have decided that it could safely ignore all this. When anyone complained that this was both a huge stress test on German society and a giant social engineering project, Merkel regally announced that if she had to apologize for 'showing a friendly face', 'then this is not my country'. In fact, just as when she ordered the *Energiewende*, or when she directed that the 'rescue' of Greece be undertaken in the form of a bailout of Greece's creditors, she had for some time been governing not like a parliamentary leader but like a president with emergency powers. Inquiries into the wisdom of her immigration policy were answered by her entourage – which in this case included all the Bundestag parties – with the claim that the mere expression of dissent 'played into the hands of the Right', a potent rhetorical device in Germany. Until Cologne, concern over the government's handling of the immigration wave was effectively suppressed.

Between September and January, Merkel's minister of the interior was left out of the loop as Merkel governed directly, using staged public appearances – press conferences, talk shows and party conventions – to cultivate the support of those in German society who saw the influx of refugees as an opportunity to demonstrate to the world their country's new friendliness. Nor did she shy away from Obama-style nationalist pathos, as when in her annual summer press conference on 31 August she let her compatriots know that 'Germany is a strong country . . . We did so many things, we can do that. We can do it, and where something gets in our way,

was ready to be signed, but this came to be seen as politically inexpedient: Alexander, *Die Getriebenen: Merkel und die Flüchtlingspolitik: Report aus dem Innern der Macht* [The Driven: Merkel and Refugee Policy: Report from the Inside of Power], Munich: Siedler, 2017.

it has to be overcome.' For six months Merkel evaded all constitut-ional and political checks and balances, enjoying the praise showered on her by, among others, *Time* magazine, which made her Person of the Year 2015, throwing in for good measure the title of Chancellor of the Free World. She was talked about as a candi-date for the Nobel Peace Prize, and even Holocaust Remembrance Day on 27 January turned into a Merkelfest when the guest speaker in the Bundestag, an Austrian writer who had survived the Holocaust, told her audience that 'this country, which eighty years ago was responsible for the worst crimes of the century, has today won the applause of the world, thanks to its open borders.'

What about Europe? And why dwell so long on the refugee crisis when I'm supposed to be discussing a book on the euro crisis?* The answer is that Merkel's immigration policy offers an object lesson in what other countries can expect from Germany acting European. Just as the United States sees the world as an extended playing field for its domestic political economy, Germany has come to consider the European Union as an extension of itself, where what is right for Germany is by definition right for all others. There is nothing particularly immoral about this; indeed most Germans think it is supremely moral, as they identify their control of Europe with a post-nationalism understood as anti-nationalism, which in turn is understood as the quintessential lesson of German history. Very much like the US, German elites project what they collectively regard as self-evident, natural and reasonable onto *their* outside world, and they are puzzled that anyone could possibly fail to see things the way they do. Do the dissenters perhaps suffer from cognitive deficits and require education by Schäuble in the Eurogroup classroom?

---

* Martin Sandbu, *Europe's Orphan: The Future of the Euro and the Politics of Debt*, Princeton, NJ: Princeton University Press, 2016.

One problem with hegemonic self-righteousness is that it prevents the self-righteous from seeing that what they consider morally self-evident may be informed by self-interest – for example, the self-interest of German export industries informing the German identification of the 'European idea' with the single European currency. The problem is exacerbated by the fact that the national interest that is mistakenly seen as identical to the interest of all reasonable human beings, in Europe and beyond, is necessarily shaped by the political interest of the government and its dominant social bloc in preserving their power. This puts peripheral countries at the mercy of the national power games and the moral and semantic ethnocentrisms of countries at the centre, which are hard to decipher for outsiders – especially with a postmodern political leader like Merkel who, free from substantive commitments and, apparently, constitutional constraints, has perfected the art of staying in power by unpredictable changes of course.

As the refugee crisis unfolded, Europe was dragged into the complicated twists and turns of German domestic politics. Merkel early on informed an astonished German public that controlling national borders had become 'impossible in the twenty-first century', and backed this up by aggressively criticizing the Hungarian government for preparing to close its borders. After Cologne, of course, the closing of borders suddenly became possible again, and Hungary re-emerged as a model for the rest of Europe, in particular for Greece, which was threatened by Germany with exclusion from the Schengen area if it didn't seal its borders. German law forbids, or is said by the German government to forbid, sending would-be immigrants away once they have expressed a desire to apply for asylum. So Merkel had to get the Greeks, and Europe as whole, to observe this principle, lest her German pro-immigration constituency smelled the rat that was heading in their direction. The burden of keeping the migrants out of Europe fell on Turkey, which was to put an end to the trafficking of migrants to Greece – on a country, that is, whose human rights record suggests that it may not be particularly careful when dealing with Syrian or any other refugees. Of course, Turkish cooperation had a price, and though Merkel had in the past steadfastly Turkey's bid for EU membership, now, having changed tack again and speaking on behalf of Europe as a whole, she promised Erdoğan expedited negotiations on accession as a reward for preventing the Syrian refugees she had invited to enter Germany from entering Greece. When Turkey demanded money as well, Merkel chose to see this as a matter for 'European solidarity', just like the funding of the new EU border protection agency, Frontex, which patrols the Greek and Italian coastlines. European borders were turned into German borders, and by implication Europe into Germany.

So immigration became 'Europeanized' for German domestic reasons. One of Merkel's highest priority became to avoid having to close the German border, as Denmark and Sweden have closed theirs: closed borders make for ugly pictures, and they also make German voters wonder why they should pay for 'Europe' if they have to stop at the German border when going on vacation. Moreover, German business began claiming that the end of Schengen would cost billions because of time lost at Europe's internal borders, as well as tens of thousands of jobs.* Even so, the German public had to be given a reason to believe that the number of immigrants coming to Germany was going to drop. EU member states therefore had to agree to take a share of the immigrants invited by Germany, even though they weren't consulted before Merkel made her offer. Moreover, the number of migrants could

---

* Enthusiasm among German employers for immigration-by-asylum had vanished. By July 2016 the thirty DAX companies had hired no more than fifty-four of the refugees of 2015 in regular jobs. Germany together with other EU member countries formally complained to the Turkish government that the very few Syrian refugees that Turkey sent to Europe under the Merkel-Erdoğan agreement were either in need of extensive medical treatment or unskilled. The Turkish government shortly thereafter confirmed that it preferred to keep academically trained Syrians in Turkey: 'European Union-Flücht-lingsdeal: Türkei lässt hochqualifizierte Syrer nicht ausreisen', [European Union Refugee Deal: Turkey Will Not Allow Highly Qualified Syrians to Leave] *Spiegel*, 21 May 2016.

have no upper limit, or *Obergrenze*, a term that Merkel's PR machine had declared anathema, upon which it become a signifier in German public discourse of *Fremdenfeindlichkeit* (xenophobia, if not racism). It is, of course, difficult for member countries to commit to letting in a defined proportion of an undefined total number of migrants. So Visegrád-bashing – Visegrád representing the alliance of four Central European countries, the Czech Republic, Poland, Slovakia and Hungary – followed Hungary-bashing, and German politicians started threatening Poland, of all countries, with financial punishment unless it fell in line with German-style 'European solidarity'.

What European solidarity involves changes rapidly and unpredictably, in the Merkel way. Confronting three critical *Länder* elections in the spring of 2016, Merkel pointed out in a speech to a CDU party meeting on 30 January that 'protection under the Geneva Convention is for the moment limited to three years'.* Refugees had to understand that their status was a temporary one, she said. Addressing them as 'Du' rather than the formal 'Sie', Merkel continued: 'We expect that, when peace will have returned to Syria and the IS in Iraq will be defeated, you will, with the skills that you will have received here, return to your homeland.' While this was designed to assuage the growing opposition to immigration and perhaps to deter some of the would-be immigrants, core supporters of *Wilkommenskultur* would still pin their hopes on the fact that in Germany refugees are normally granted indefinite leave to remain after three years, and only a tiny number are sent back to their countries of origin even if, after lengthy legal procedures, it's decided that they haven't got grounds to remain.

The result of all this equivocation, double-talk and Merkel-speak, of a difficult-to-disentangle amalgam of self-interest and

---

*   On 13 March 2016 elections were held in Baden-Württemberg, Rheinland-Pfalz and Sachsen-Anhalt. The AfD received 15, 13 and 24 per cent of the vote, respectively, and established itself as a new element of the German party system.

sentimentality, is an immense political and institutional mess – a product of a German domestic politics that has become volatile and unpredictable. European institutions serve as transmission belts for imposing on other European countries German policies enlarged to become European policies to which, supposedly, there is no alternative. This includes a restructuring of the citizenry through immigration, not just in Germany where it might seem economically or demographically expedient, but also in other European countries where it is not. No consideration was given to the diverse labour market and political conditions in the countries expected to take in fixed shares of migrants, among them countries with high birth rates (Poland, Ireland), weak labour markets (Spain), and highly uncertain economic perspectives (Italy). The result of this sort of decision-making is rapidly rising anti-German sentiment in the form of anti-European sentiment, not only among political elites but also, most powerfully, among electorates. In response, ever more political and economic muscle is being applied by the German government to the rest of Europe in the belief that this is unfortunately required to save Europe from total collapse.

Devastation has similarly been visited on the Economic and Monetary Union (EMU): German-dictated European solutions to the debt and growth crisis have led to economic and political disaster. As with immigration, pressure is building in European countries for more national autonomy on economic policy, including monetary policy. There is growing interest in a 'Plan B' for the euro, in case attempts by France and Italy in particular to force Germany and its allies into a non-German 'European solution' do not succeed. The new 'European question' is whether Europe must put up forever with having to follow the vagaries of German domestic politics – and if there are ways to protect Europe from the antics of the latter dismantling centralized European institutions such as Dublin, Schengen and the euro.

This is, finally, where Martin Sandbu's refreshingly eccentric book comes in. Its argument, in short, is that giving up on monetary union would be a mistake, since a common European currency, unlike what Europeans are being told, does not have to be a common German currency requiring a common German political economy. The euro, Sandbu argues, leaves enough space for national variety, autonomy and democracy. That the EMU is in such deplorable condition is the result of ill-conceived policy decisions made as a consequence of German hegemony, abetted by French opportunism and collective strategic short-sightedness. According to Sandbu, a self-confessed European federalist of Spinellian inspiration, the euro is needed, both by Europe and the world, but could be better governed than it is today, if it was governed on British rather than German terms, which would safeguard national sovereignty regardless of the common supranational currency. To top it all off, Sandbu argues that Britain should not only remain in the EU but should adopt the euro, the sooner the better, in its own interest as well as that of Europe and everybody else.

Sandbu's book is both retrospective and forward-looking; its author, small wonder given that he works for the *Financial Times*, is enviably certain that he knows exactly what went wrong with the euro and how it could be fixed. He offers a scathing critique of European 'rescue policies' after 2008, presenting them as Germany's imposition of its national interests and ideology on the rest of Europe. A Monday-morning quarterback if there ever was one, he expounds at length on what the mistakes were, and why they were made. One needs some patience here, until one begins to see that Sandbu does in fact have a point: a bail-in of those that had hoped to profit from high-risk lending to what became 'debtor countries' might have spared Europe many of the political divisions, the infringements on national sovereignty and national democracy, the debt bondage and the economic agony that Euroland countries have had to suffer so that banks and their shareholders and creditors could be bailed out.

In developing his argument, Sandbu offers an interestingly revisionist account of the post-2008 European crisis. According to him, it was not caused by anything specific to the euro but by a credit bubble that affected most rich capitalist countries at the turn of the century. In Europe the bubble was caused by surplus countries under German leadership moving their capital from north to south. That this turned out to be so devastating was due to national policies in the debtor countries allowing the credit furnished by reckless lenders to be used for consumption instead of improving productivity. Sandbu argues that debtor countries like Greece and Spain did not have a 'competitiveness problem', the diagnosis of creditor countries and international organizations, but suffered simply from overconsumption made possible by borrowed money. The national governments, which together with imprudent banks had produced the bubble, could and should have been left to deal with the consequences on their own, by way of debt restructuring and bank resolution followed by structural reform and fiscal expansion. Instead, creditor countries bailed out debtor countries so they would be able to service the debt, which was held mostly by German and French financial institutions. In return, they expected austerity policies that were intended to increase national competitiveness but in fact merely stifled growth.

Sandbu attributes the insistence on austerity to Germany's 'moral' obsessions, according to which debt must always be repaid in full come what may – he sides with the 'mad Germans' rather than the 'bad Germans' theory. This relieves him of the need to address the possibility that Germany, and other countries as well, may have been afraid that risk premiums on public debt would increase in response to creditors having to accept 'haircuts' – an increase that would pose problems for indebted countries where servicing that debt consumes a significant share of public expenditure.

Looking forward, Sandbu argues that a common monetary regime is possible without creating a situation in which the Germans run it while other countries resist until, as with the immigration crisis, we end up with a costly stand-off. National sovereignty, Sandbu claims, is compatible with monetary union;

no centralized control is required. In particular, there is no need for flexible exchange rates between European countries however different they may be, or for debt mutualization. Moreover, under the umbrella of the common currency there is leeway for voluntary coalitions of the willing and able – for groups of countries to issue eurobonds, for example, with or without German participation, just as clusters of countries are currently coming together to replace the defunct Schengen regime. Even if there was a problem with competitiveness, which in countries with monetary sovereignty would normally be resolved by monetary devaluation, fiscal devaluation could do the trick, with governments cutting non-wage labour costs and borrowing to fill the resulting fiscal gap.

Of course, Sandbu's optimism depends on the German government convincing itself and its voters to abandon its 'idolatry of debt', and resisting American pressure to protect American loans and banks. Sandbu wants the Germans to learn from the British that lending is a practice to which *caveat emptor* applies: a bank that extends credit to overindebted governments or to firms and consumers unlikely to repay it must bear the consequences – there should be no bailing out of imprudent lenders under the guise of international solidarity. Other conditions that must be met include the Germans ceding their role as international disciplinarians to the financial markets; the French giving up their belief that states are smarter than banks, and getting rid of their 'vainglory and the lack of confidence that so often underpins it'; and the British abandoning their obsession with 'balancing' the European powers and joining the EMU to prevent Germany from establishing itself as the European unifier (and in so doing blowing up the European construction). In addition, countries lagging in productivity must under the pressure of now more risk-conscious financial markets impose the domestic reforms necessary for nationally generated fiscal stimulus to work – the very reforms that German-cum-European pressure has up until now been unable to bring about in the face of popular and elite resistance. Inflation-prone national institutions, especially wage-setting regimes, must be converted into productivity-enhancing ones, and democratically elected governments must resist the temptation to allow credit to be spent on consumption. Behind Sandbu's scenario for a wonderful tomorrow under the EMU, one senses an economist's lack of appreciation for the inertia of institutions, social structures and established ways of life, as well as an overly generous view of the capacity of markets to punish and correct political opportunism, and of treasuries to govern and restructure economies and societies using skilfully measured doses of money and credit – a dream Keynes may be forgiven for having dreamed in a society incomparably more deferential to established authority than today's.

Sandbu's belief that a common European currency can be run without an international hierarchy given to 'unforced (or German-forced) errors' is fair enough. But can we ignore the politics here – the relation of the German government to its electorate, of northern states in relation to their southern and eastern peripheries, and of southern elites requiring infusions of cash to prevent their states and societies from falling apart? And *can* markets be trusted to make politics dispensable? Even if the debt crisis is, as Sandbu suggests, resolved by sovereign default and debt forgiveness, and if some kind of growth can be restored by a politics of productivity instead of debt-financed consumption – will this close the gap between incomes and living standards in the European North and South and thereby pre-empt demands for a 'transfer union'? There is certainly room for doubt: consider the apparently insurmountable regional disparities between northern and southern Italy, or between West Germany and East Germany, where another non-optimal currency union took place twenty-five years ago. Unlike the disparity between north and south in Italy, the German regional income gap cannot be blamed on mafioso malfeasance. Nor was there a lack of 'reform' in East Germany: the old elite there was removed in 1990 for a comprehensive transfer of the West German system. Still, for almost two decades now, per capita income in East Germany has been between 25 and 30 per cent lower than in the West, and tax revenue is lower still, even though, since the turn of the century, there has been a yearly transfer from west to east of between 3 and 4 per cent of national GDP. All this does, however, is keep the gap from widening.

Sandbu's vision of a prosperous future under a common currency, with national autonomy benevolently policed by a well-ordered financial market, may seem an economist's utopia. National interests and national institutions may not as easily be rectified by financial markets as Sandbu appears to believe. Whether monetary union will break down like Dublin and Schengen remains to be seen; a common currency is certainly stickier than a common border regime. What seems most likely, unfortunately, is a big and long-lasting mess. National autonomy and sovereignty will be at the centre of a succession of indecisive battles over the meaning of European treaties, the political role and legal jurisdiction of the European Central Bank, the content of new reform packages, and the size of the transfers to which reforming countries will be entitled – all this accompanied by growing popular alienation and voter discontent. The North will threaten to starve the South, the South will gang up on the North, Germany will undertake to 'reform' France, France will demand 'European solidarity' from Germany. There will be a decade of bad blood, mutual incrimination, temporary fixes and ever-declining respect for centrist parties, national governments and international institutions. It will be nasty, brutish and unfortunately far from short.

PART III

Ideas

CHAPTER 11

Fighting the State

May 2019

NEOLIBERALISM, WE LEARN FROM this truly eye-opening book, is not new at all; it is, in fact, almost a century old.* Why 'neo', then? Because it was conceived and intended to promote the return of the stateless liberal *Weltwirtschaft* (the globally integrated world economy of the gold standard), which even Karl Polanyi sometimes celebrated with a note of nostalgia. Conceived it was by an identifiable, and now precisely identified, group of people who carried it and the project it stood for to its victory, however preliminary, in our time. The end of liberalism and the rise of neoliberalism began in 1918, with the fall of the empires of free trade and their replacement with a host of sovereign and potentially democratic nation-states, carriers of a dangerous virus called 'economic nationalism'. After 1945 followed decolonization and the introduction of majority voting in the General Assembly of the United Nations – anti-liberal political architectures which, together with the Keynesian gospel of national self-sufficiency, threatened not just economic progress

---

* Quinn Slobodian, *Globalists: The End of Empire and the Birth of Neoliberalism*, Cambridge, MA: Harvard University Press, 2018.

but also, this was the claim, the open society, human freedom and dignity. Hence the prefix 'neo'.

Contemporary literature on neoliberalism works with many, more or less mutually compatible definitions, and there is no need to discard any of them out of hand. Still, in the sense in which Slobodian pursues the concept back to its origins, we can now use it with much more confidence and precision. Neoliberalism, in short, is about the desirability and possibility of a return to a kind of liberal cosmopolitanism that Adam Smith described in his analysis of the rise of capitalism (in other words, the ownership of 'stock') in an early modern, still borderless Europe:

> The proprietor of stock is necessarily a citizen of the world, and is not necessarily attached to any particular country. He would be apt to abandon the country in which he was exposed to a vexatious inquisition, in order to be assessed to a burdensome tax, and would remove his stock to some other country where he could either carry on his business, or enjoy his fortune more at his ease. (*The Wealth of Nations:* IV–V, 1776, p. 442)

Restoring stock owners' cosmopolitan paradise required sophisticated intellectual, ideological and institutional manoeuvres – the relentless, untiring invention of ever-new tactical moves in pursuit of a never-changing strategy. The long list of neoliberalism's conceptual props and related political strategies included distinguishing between public imperium and private dominium and raising the latter, as a basic human right, above the former; making different states adopt identical laws guaranteeing private property rights ('isonomy'); implanting so-called 'xenos rights' in national constitutions granting foreigners the same economic rights that they enjoy at home; the internationalization of private law or the substitution of international private for national public law; international federations of states guaranteeing international peace while having to have a liberal economic order due to their internal heterogeneity; and common markets encompassing collections of states and obliging them to allow for unlimited competition between and within their economies, through free movement of goods and services, as well as, importantly, capital and, perhaps, labour – as enshrined in the 1990s by the European Union, in the form of the 'four freedoms' of its internal market. From the beginning, the outlook was decidedly global and in this sense universalistic; anything particularistic, like national states, was and is considered to be a threat to the grand design of a borderless *Weltwirtschaft* that was expected to restore the golden age of unbounded nineteenth-century liberalism.

Not that all other definitions of neoliberalism would be rendered obsolete by Slobodian's history of the neoliberal idea.* Most of them, however, more or less deal with social and cultural adjustments to the structural condition of protected property and unprotected societies that the globalizers had in mind (and have, if perhaps only temporarily, been able to shepherd into being) – that is with the base, if one wants to call it such, on which the superstructure of neoliberal culture, the 'economization' and the competitive individualism of contemporary social life, has grown. Indeed, it is only by reading Slobodian that we can fully understand the particular relationship of neoliberalism to the modern nation-state, which is one of opposition and dependence at the same time – opposition to its inherent tendencies to contain and thereby distort markets, and dependence on its sovereign capacity to fend off and suppress social demands for protection that would

---

* There are quite a few of them. An inevitably incomplete selection includes Cornel Ban, *Ruling Ideas: How Global Neoliberalism Goes Local* (2016), Johanna Bockman, *Markets in the Name of Socialism: The Left-wing Origins of Neoliberalism* (2011), Wendy Brown, *Undoing the Demos: Neoliberalism's Stealth Revolution* (2015), Pierre Dardot and Christian Laval, *The New Way of the World: On Neoliberal Society* (2013), Gérard Duménil and Dominique Lévy, *Capital Resurgent: Roots of the Neoliberal Revolution* (2004), Michel Foucault, *The Birth of Biopolitics: Lectures at the Collège de France, 1978–1979* (2008) and Martijn Konings, *Capital and Time: For a New Critique of Neoliberal Reason* (2018).

de-liberalize the economy. The task is to weaken the nation-state as an agent of economic redistribution while strengthening it as a bulwark against the illiberal dispositions of an economically unenlightened public. The critical problem here, obviously, is democracy with its inevitably egalitarian bias, the illusions it spreads about the possibility of social justice, and its tendency to deteriorate into *economic* democracy at the expense of the minority of capital movers and profit shakers upon which the progress of humanity depends. Democracy must therefore be institutionalized in a way that prevents it from extending into domains where it does not belong, while the state must be able to patrol and enforce the institutional limits to democracy that alone make it compatible with a free economy. On this point, as on many others, Friedrich Hayek comes in with his constitutional designs, so often ridiculed, of a de-economized democracy in a deeply economistic political economy – institutional utopias that are succeeded today by the liberal rhetoric of the old, centrist-globalist 'cartel parties' and their mass media against 'populism' and its claim to democratic power for the purpose of distorting the free markets of neoliberal capitalism.

On a more general level, Slobodian's book helps us clarify the critical, so often misrepresented, relationship between democracy and capitalism, and the nature of neoliberalism's fragile settlement between the two. The globalists always knew that at bottom, democracy and capitalism are deadly enemies: there is no way you can have democracy under capitalism unless you manage to install a secure firewall between the two, protecting capitalism from democratic meddling. Democracy, inevitably national, can coexist with capitalism as long, and only as long, as it is restricted to the cultivation of folkloristic passions untainted by particularistic interests of class or country. Culture wars over marriage for all, passionate as they may become, are fine as long as free trade and private property in capital remain sacred. Neoliberalism, Slobodian makes clear, does not consist of releasing the capitalist economy from the state so that it can function unimpeded according to its own laws. Instead, as he puts it, liberalization means 'encasing' capitalism in state-policed institutions so that democracy cannot get to it. While this is a welcome clarification of the nature of a process that is all too often described as one of liberation – of 'market forces' but also of society as a whole – one might find it more appropriate to use the encasement metaphor for democracy rather than for the economy, with locking in, and indeed locking up, applying to democratic politics, thus preventing them from getting anywhere close to free markets and private property.

Slobodian describes the history of neoliberalism, of its doctrine and politics, as that of a group of extraordinary people – the 'globalizers': all men, densely 'networked' in space and time, in an era in which networking had not yet been invented. Self-renewing over three generations, the group held together from the end of World War I in 1918 to the creation of the World Trade Organization (WTO) in the 1990s, the high point of the rise, or return, of global capitalism. From a sociology of knowledge to a sociology of power, the history Slobodian relates is indispensable, not least for our understanding of what happened to capitalism and capitalist society in the twentieth century. Although Slobodian rightly attributes importance to the people whose story he recounts, he avoids falling into the traps of conspiracy theory without, however, implying that there cannot be historically potent conspiracies in the real world. Such conspiracies can make history, provided that the conspirators know how to play their game, in this case a game with and between institutional positions and resources in national politics, international organizations and academia. Slobodian's globalizers were both academics and men of affairs, but academics who understood that a theory can become historically true only if it is connected to the commanding heights of politics and the economy, where power comes into its own in being exercised over the real world in cold blood.

The organizational history of neoliberalism is long and impressive, encompassing the succession of social organisms that it temporarily inhabited until it moved on to even more conducive environments. It extends from the Austrian to the International Chamber of Commerce, and from there to the rich organizational ecology of international institutions and their headquarters and research centres in Geneva, the capital of early globalism. There a university was on hand to nurture the young and provide employment to like-minded scholars from all over, including liberal émigrés from nearby Germany. All of this was close to and easily observable from Mont Pèlerin where, after World War II, Hayek assembled his sponsors and followers for his, initially hopelessly uphill, battle against Keynesianism and social democracy. Again, one cannot help but be impressed with how conscious the leaders of what Slobodian refers to as the 'Geneva School' were of the need for a firm grounding in institutional positions of power, as well as in the media and the public mind, if they were ultimately to make the world liberal again. To prevail, a long view had to be taken, and in bad times one had to go into hiding and suffer isolation and even ridicule, without letting oneself be consumed with self-doubt or despair. The only apt comparison would be with the Bolsheviks under Lenin, who were revolutionaries with a similarly stoic self-confidence and who were in many ways the only serious competitors of Hayek and his combatants until their final defeat in 1989.

Slobodian's globalizers were a sect, slowly turning into a church, of Gramscian 'organic intellectuals' the likes of which the Left has never been able to produce post-Gramsci. This was certainly true after the 1960s when world capitalism began dismantling the economic constitution of the post-war settlement in which it was kept confined as punishment for the deadly disorder it had wrought in the first half of the century. There are no indications of the sect and their leaders ever having been shaken by doubts about the world-historical significance of their mission, leaving them unwaveringly hopeful even in dire defeat, which they took as an opportunity to learn and regroup. Organizing was the basis of it all: seminars, meetings, university departments, collective publications, prizes for the young, making connections with sponsors while themselves sponsoring whoever might at some point prove worthy of co-optation and adoption. Differences in theory were allowed, within limits, as long as they did not call forth differences in practice, and theories were flexibly adjusted to changing circumstances. Extensive rotation between academia and politics, between theory and practice, was the very essence of neoliberal organization; for this the almost indefinite number of organizations and institutions around Geneva was available for acolytes of Hayek's Mont Pèlerin Society (MPS) to be placed, enriching not just them but, more importantly, the treasure of experience collectively accumulated within their brotherhood. In the end the Geneva globalizers commanded a huge number of institutions dispersed throughout the entire Western world – from the Rockefeller Foundation in New York to the GATT in Geneva and the Max Planck Institute in Hamburg. All were skilfully instrumentalized in the service of defeating the democratic nation-state as a would-be governor of a capitalist economy moved outside its reach by means of 'globalization'.

Among the many fascinating things we learn from Slobodian is the prominence of German and Austrian internationalist economists among the early globalizers, plausibly owing to their particularly painful experience after 1918 with the destruction of market-liberal empires in favour of national, and often outright democratic, statehood. We also learn how early the Right understood the full implications of the fundamental conflict between capitalism and democracy while parts of the Left were still dreaming of an international capitalism with a 'social dimension', if not a human face. Readers also learn about the closeness, above and beyond all factional disputes, between German ordoliberals of all stripes and colours and the Geneva globalizers on the one hand, and Carl Schmitt's authoritarian, strong-state anti-liberalism and anti-democratism on the other: from the globalists' global perspective the commonalities clearly outweighed the differences. In fact, far from being isolated in their defeated country, Germany's post-war ordoliberals, from Franz Böhm to Wilhelm Röpke, were a major force at the international, 'Geneva' level, just as they were surprisingly effective contributors to the rise of anti–New Deal neoliberalism in the United States, which began as early as the 1950s. Those less familiar with intellectual history may also wonder about the deep involvement in neoliberal organizing and politics of someone like Ludwig von Mises, one of the great theoretical economists of his age. A market-liberal if there ever was one, he died in 1973 at the age of ninety-two, in New York where, as Slobodian reveals, he had for decades lived in a rent-controlled apartment on the Upper West Side.

Even more exciting is Slobodian's story about the European integration project. Initially 'Europe' was contested among the neoliberals, since it was not global in reach and might evolve into a regional superstate interrupting the free flow of goods, services and capital in the *Weltwirtschaft*. This would become the political line of Margaret Thatcher and later that of some of the Brexiteers in 2016. But others saw the European Union, in its successive incorporations, as a model of how to tame the democratic nation-state through a legally enshrined supranational market, one with guaranteed property rights and an anti-interventionist competition law. That model combined isonomy and supranational law enforced by an international court with direct effect in national systems, thereby circumventing national legal and political systems and making them run dry – all of this building on and developing further the Hayekian federation project of the 1930s and 1940s. Even to someone who had already pointed out at length the affinity of Hayekian federalism with the European construction as of the early 2000s,* it was amazing to see how central the idea of a

---

* See Streeck, *Buying Time: The Delayed Crisis of Democratic Capitalism*, London and New York: Verso, 2014.

federation of maximally diverse countries once was to neoliberal globalism, with a free world market promoted as the price, like it or not, for international peace. Before Slobodian, it was not in any way clear to the political scientist how extensive and forward-looking construction of the neoliberal project was from early on – to be precise, from the late 1930s, on the eve of another global war. When German ordoliberals, driven from Bonn where Konrad Adenauer despised them because of their ideological inflexibility, went to Brussels to help design the legal and institutional architecture of an integrated 'Europe', they were able to bring with them long-thought-through institutional blueprints whose practical consequences and intentions hardly anyone understood apart from themselves.

Among many other things, Slobodian's book teaches us the importance of intellectual history, both for the production of new knowledge and the education of future scholars. As we read, one conceptual piece after the other falls into place and thereby reveals deep connections and connotations that we might otherwise overlook. One case in point, and only one among many, is the astonishing continuity and inner coherence of the life's work of a true polymath like Friedrich August von Hayek, on the economy, on politics, on social institutions, and on knowledge and on its origins and uses – held together by an underlying problem-cum-project that kept evolving with the historical situation and the political opportunities and constraints it entailed. Beginning with Hayek's involvement in the Viennese debates in the 1920s about socialist planning and its limits, debates in which Joseph Schumpeter and Karl Polanyi also participated, it continued in the 1930s, on the eve of World War II, as Hayek wrote about international federations that were to secure world peace while, disguised as a by-product, safely enshrining a liberal economy. Shortly before this, Hayek had dissociated himself from *Konjunkturforschung* (the econometric and mathematical study of the business cycle), which he found too akin to Keynesian ambitions to 'steer' the economy, letting the world know in no uncertain terms that Professor Keynes unfortunately did not have the faintest idea about economics. As Slobodian writes, Hayek himself declared the capitalist market economy to be 'sublime' and beyond human comprehension, something to be left to itself and that one interferes with at one's own risk. Hence Hayek's turn to institutionalism and the theorizing of institutional change, with an emphasis on the stickiness of institutions and the need to restrict human intervention in them to 'gardening' rather than 'design'. This did not prevent him from developing wide-ranging, utopian ideas about the right kind of political institutions for (neo)liberal political economies, institutions designed to keep politics out of markets and protect the unknowable economy from the necessarily inept intervention in its majestic sublime self-organization by under-educated social-democratic majorities aspiring to such presumptuous objectives as social justice.

From here, at the culmination of his career as one of the most politically influential thinkers of the twentieth century, Hayek arrived at his theory of 'complexity', drawing on neuropsychology and general system theory. To him this delivered the ultimate proof of the futility, and indeed frivolity, of any human attempt collectively to intervene in the course of human history, economic or otherwise, with the exception, obviously, of himself and his MPS combatants. Complexity theory à la Hayek in effect managed to defend an aristocratic social order, deeply rooted in the capitalist nature of the modern political economy, in which equality is not an end but, at best, a means to discover the very few who, by coming out on top, prove themselves to be the only ones who matter. While Hayekianism has long become the working hypothesis of neoliberalized capitalism, until now nobody has dared to draw out its implications with the frankness and the courage of its originator, and it is to Slobodian's great merit that he helps us see the connection between the admirable scholarship, on the one hand, and the sinister political project driving it, on the other.

Hayek's theory of complexity, so much more sophisticated than what his fellows were able to deliver, was from its beginnings conceived to frustrate democratic-egalitarian 'socialism' and to ensure that the world continued to operate according to the market principle of cumulative advantage, as summed up in, of all places, the King James Bible: 'For unto every one that hath shall be given, and he shall have abundance: but from him that hath not shall be taken even that which he hath' (Matthew 25:29). This, Hayek believed, and the neoliberals dutifully took from him, was still unendingly better than social-democratic tampering with the mysteries of a hyper-complex global capitalism. There was no discussion that one might perhaps want to look for ways of de-composing a global complexity that escapes governability, and in return gain something like democratic self-determination and collective fate control.

An interesting question which Slobodian does not touch on – and which indeed is strictly speaking not his subject – is the extent to which today's Left has bought into globalist doctrine. By the 1990s, Third Way social democracy had come to accept as dogma that 'globalization', meaning open markets in an integrated world economy, was not just inevitable but outright desirable; that 'economic nationalism' was evil; and that it was the new, perhaps the last remaining, mission of nation-states to open up their economies and societies to global competition while help-ing their citizens, within the bounds of the possible, adjust to a continuously and inescapably changing world. Recently, 'economic nationalism' has also become public enemy number one for a more radically internationalist non-centrist Left. That Left rallies behind a 'no border' programme it believes to be anti-capitalist, unaware that the abolition of the nation-state is a dream that capitalists have dreamed of long before them. Several times in his book, Slobodian tries to draw a line between pro-capitalist and anti-capitalist anti-nationalism by intimating that, while his globalists on the surface professed to adhere to the same four freedoms as, for example, the British Remainers, in fact, racist as they were, they did not take the fourth freedom seriously and allowed for countries limiting or wholesale prohibiting inward migration.

Were the globalists racist? In a fascinating chapter, Slobodian explores how someone like Wilhelm Röpke, an outspoken opponent of Nazi Germany's anti-Semitism, who had to emigrate after Hitler's seizure of power (*Machtergreifung*), identified with the most disgusting racist tropes to justify South African apartheid and denounce decolonialization and majority voting in the United Nations. But although Röpke was joined in this by some of his colleagues from the MPS, Slobodian concedes that at the end this was a minority position. The globalizers' overriding goal was to abolish, if not the nation-state, then its political capacity, by exposing it to a competitive world economy with safely enshrined property rights. Anything that could provoke popular opposition to this had to take second place. If immigration on a large scale threatened to wake up sleeping democratic dogs, one had better not push it. But this was for wholly pragmatic reasons, on condition that competition in global markets for goods, services and capital sufficed to do the trick and reduce nation-states to sites for patriotic flag-waving nostalgia. Failing this, immigration across open borders as a universal human right under international law was kept in reserve, as an additional means to soften up national solidarity by importing the international market for labour into the national political economy. When it came down to the capitalist basics, the practical men from the MPS not only abandoned 'racist' objections to 'multiculturalism' and the like, but denounced them with much the same rhetoric as their apparent opponents on the noncentrist radical Left.*

---

*. Today this seems truer than ever. As the de-legitimation of economic nationalism by pointing to the alleged benefits of free trade has got stuck and the

A case in point here is the third-generation Geneva-type globalizer Peter Sutherland, a multifunctionary of capital, who was among many other things a member of the European Commission (1985–89), the founding director of the WTO (1993–95), and chairman of Goldman Sachs International (1995–2015). Sutherland, a lawyer from Ireland, briefly appears in Slobodian's account. Giving, as director designate of the WTO, the Third Hayek Memorial Lecture (1994), Sutherland let it be known that the new organization was based on 'two of Hayek's key insights – the role of the price system in conveying information and the importance of the rule of law'. Slobodian also mentions Sutherland's activities as European commissioner in charge of competition. In this capacity, according to Slobodian, 'his activism earned him the nickname "the sheriff" from Jacques Delors, because he used competition law aggressively to liberalize trade within the European Community and bring individual nations to the European Court of Justice. One scholar', Slobodian continues, 'calls him the "embodiment of neoliberal ideas in the European Commission" as he used the European Court of Justice to end state funding of national industries and ramp up competition'.

Even more prominently, Sutherland became an activist for unrestricted immigration. As the United Nations Special Representative for International Migration (from 2006 until his death in 2017), Sutherland called upon the European Union to 'do its best to undermine the homogeneity of its member states – however difficult it may be to explain this to the citizens of those states'. The objective, as stated in an article written by Sutherland with the then European commissioner for home affairs, Cecilia Malmström, was national or European

spectre of national protectionism is raising its anti-liberal head, now the abolishment of national borders is increasingly being framed as an internationalist moral obligation, with economic nationalists being denounced as xenophobes at best.

'competitiveness'.* 'During the Arab revolutions', said Sutherland and Malmström, 'the EU missed a historic opportunity to begin weaving together the two sides of the Mediterranean'.† Today, only a few years later, technocratic population engineering from above has become politically unsustainable – exactly like the WTO's brave new free trade world after Seattle – due to popular resistance dubbed 'populist', or indeed 'racist', not just by the neoliberals but also by their left-liberal comrades-in-arms and the no-border radical Left. Now, even the more intelligent opportunists from the 1990s like Lawrence 'Larry' Summers, who was treasury secretary under Bill Clinton, are calling for a new, 'responsible' nationalism that includes managed trade to ensure that the benefits of open markets are more equally distributed both between and within participating countries. This begs the question whether freedom of movement of labour, the fourth of the four transnational freedoms of the neoliberal utopia, can, should and must remain standing when the three others are being pulled back into the ambit of democratic-national politics. It also raises the issue of whether socially and economically heterogeneous countries exposed to free immigration can muster the political will to fight internal inequality by protecting their societies from the vagaries of global markets. Can a country re-establish 'economic nationalism' without having control over immigration? Table 1 offers a simplified classification of different politics regarding the 'four freedoms', in terms of the four possible combinations of positions on the free movement of labour with the free movement of goods, services, and capital.

---

*   Although one does find Sutherland advocating free immigration also as a human right of the migrant, not subject to restrictions for economic reasons on the part of receiving countries. From 2015 on, Sutherland served as president of the International Catholic Migration Commission, making him a close adviser to the Holy See.

†   Peter D. Sutherland and Cecilia Malmström, 'Europe's Immigration Challenge', *Guardian*, 24 July 2012.

TABLE I

The Politics of the Four Freedoms

	Free movement of goods, services, capital	*Free movement of labour*
Neoliberals ('Remainers')	Keep	Keep
No-border Left	Suspend (?)	Keep
Liberal Centrists ('Soft Brexit')	Keep	Suspend
Economic Nationalists ('Full Brexit')	Suspend	Suspend

After reading this exciting book, scholars who have spent part or all of their careers studying 'European integration' may want to take a step back and reflect. As wilfully neutered academics, they have for decades conscientiously analysed, applied, defined and redefined, stretched and narrowed down concepts such as multi-level government, global governance, public choice, complexity, subsidiarity and the like, taking them seriously on their face value and turning them into fashionable intellectual toys of a presentist social science entirely untroubled by its political irrelevance. Now they can understand the source of those toys that came to them: from a political programme so old and established that its insiders could talk about it without mentioning it. Here there was a consciousness of purpose, a desire to make history, that was so entirely alien to a stable-fed, domesticated academy, both set free and cut off from political-social responsibility, that its theories were unable to recognize it. Compared to Slobodian's globalists, the army of political scientists that specialized, mostly with funding from Brussels, in debating intergovernmentalism versus neofunctionalism, must appear hopelessly out of step with the contemporary world around them. Indeed only a few of them, if any, ever cared about the context in which the Hayeks of this world – and how very worldly they were! – had originated concepts such as 'integration by law' or 'global governance', a context from which such concepts derived their specific spin defining them in a more than lexicographic sense, that is, in the sense that matters. Academic social science gratefully received them, as it were, as free gifts, cut off from their moorings, as innocent analytical constructs, *l'art pour l'art*, to be used as chips in value-free *Glasperlenspiele* (glass bead games) leading to comfortably paid, preferably tenured academic employment.

With hindsight, thanks to Slobodian, it is easy to see, although probably prohibitively uncomfortable to realize, what happened here. The 'globalizers' of Geneva and the Mont Pèlerin Society and their audience understood what they were talking about, so well that they did not always have to be explicit about it, whereas their academic epigones had no idea from which table the breadcrumbs had fallen that they spent their lives chewing on. That table was, of course, the one where the possibility of global capitalism in a world of mass democracy was being explored and denied – an issue of which the invited guests were viscerally conscious. This was not true for those deep down in their Platonian cave, where they were reduced to staring at the shadows on the PowerPoint wall in front of them, cut off from the ideas that produced them and believing capitalism to have happily been parcelled out to some other 'discipline' so that they fortunately didn't have to bother with it. Taken out of context, however, their concepts, whose origins and history they wouldn't know because they thought them irrelevant, became entirely arbitrary; they could mean whatever one attributed to them. To avoid attracting the disapproving eye of the next appointment committee, attributed meanings were typically nice and pleasant, that is, cleansed of any association with capitalism. 'Integration'? Good for peace. 'Social dimension'? A human face for the market. 'The four freedoms'? A better life for all, now or later. Capitalism was for the economists and their in any case too difficult mathematics – not noting that the globalizers themselves had long given up on economics, except as a propaganda tool for enlightening the unwashed about their real 'needs', austerity now for prosperity later. They had moved on to the law and political institution building as their ultimate instruments to neutralize politics and, in a world of democratic states dangerously prone to using their powers to improve the lot of the many at the expense of the few, turn the state into the Great Protector of capitalism.

CHAPTER 12

Wrong Ideas or Real Interests?

February 2015

IN POLITICS, WHAT IS more important, ideas or interests? Mark Blyth, professor of international political economy at Brown University in Providence, Rhode Island, decided early on that ideas have primacy. Politics, according to Blyth, may be right or wrong, but cannot be right if shaped by wrong ideas. Wrong ideas can become obsessions; eliminating them calls for science as well as for rhetoric. Blyth delivers both in his impressive book.*

The false *idée fixe* from which Blyth would like to liberate the world is that of 'austerity' as the royal road out of capitalist crises. Austerity means cutting back the state in favour of the market, downsizing the public in favour of the private sector, and reducing government debt by lowering government expenditure. In short, it advocates public thrift so as to increase private prosperity. Blyth wishes to demonstrate that this is a 'dangerous idea'. He begins with an account of the financial and fiscal crisis of 2008 as the crisis of a deregulated banking system and, thereafter, of public

---

* Mark Blyth, *Austerity: The History of a Dangerous Idea*, Oxford: Oxford University Press, 2013.

finances. He follows this up with an intellectual history of austerity politics as the history first of liberalism, starting with Locke, Hume and Smith, and then of neoliberalism, especially of the Austrian School, German ordoliberalism and the latest macroeconomics. He then provides a factual history of the failure of austerity politics in the twentieth and twenty-first centuries, from the return to the gold standard in the 1920s, via the world depression and on to the Europe of today. The book ends with an outline of a crisis therapy which would avoid the pains of austerity.

Blyth's book is well written; it is comprehensible and on occasion entertaining, without making concessions to the reader. This holds good for the intellectual history, which traces the long development of the austerity project and its astonishing theoretical assumptions right down to the Italian School of Einaudi and Bocconi (including Mario Monti!) with its enormous influence on European mainstream and international politics. The same is true of the factual history, which can be read as an introduction to the crisis history of modern capitalism and the theoretical and political history accompanying it. Of particular interest is Blyth's highly informative and at the same time amusingly polemical discussion of those countries in which, according to the neoliberal crisis-fighters, austerity is supposed to have led to growth ('expansionary fiscal consolidation'). Those countries include the victims of the 'Washington consensus' in the global South as well as the Baltic states, Bulgaria and Romania (dubbed the REBLLs by Blyth). It is entertaining to watch Blyth dismantle the propaganda writings, camouflaged as 'science', of both star and standard economists, to find confirmation of his claim that 'austerity is a dangerous idea' that cannot work.

As far as theory is concerned, Blyth travels light. He doesn't really aspire to get beyond Keynes's 'paradox of thrift': if an individual sees her income decline and she 'increases her savings', she may later be better off; if everyone suffers from declining incomes and they all 'save' more, especially if they are forced to do so by their governments, they will soon all be even worse off. This suffices to explain why austerity is a bad idea, especially when you compare it with the truly bizarre 'theoretical' assumptions of neoliberal macroeconomics. The bar is raised when Blyth has to explain why such an obviously absurd idea as 'growth by consolidation' has been able to enjoy such resounding success in today's Europe. Here Blyth, the critic of macroeconomics, gives way to Blyth, the theoretician of ideas, who offers us a very Anglo-Saxon view of Germany; more precisely, of a specifically German delusion. This begins with the austerity policy of the Reich government at the end of Weimar Republic, implemented with the support of the SPD and organized labour, and continues with ordoliberalism's distrust of an economically active interventionist state. Today, mediated by the Austrian School, this blends in well with the neoliberalism of the anti-Keynesian wing of US politics and the public choice school of institutional economics. Somehow or other, according to Blyth, ordoliberalism has entered the bloodstream of the Germans to the point where they regard it as a self-evident truth, and he does not shrink from illustrating this with the tired old popular etymology conflating debts [*Schulden*] with guilt [*Schuld*] and presenting Chancellor Merkel as – what else? – the archetypically thrifty 'Swabian housewife'.

Blyth's critique of austerity as idea and as instrument comes in handy for Germans who wish to help Europe recover through 'Keynesian' growth programmes, dissociating themselves from 'typically German' obsessions with stability and consolidation, in the hope of using 'Europe' to turn German political economy from its ordoliberal head onto Keynesian feet firmly planted on the ground of demand-side economics. I am referring here to those parts of the Left, close to the unions and the SPD, that conveniently forget that the SPD has steadfastly supported Merkel's European policy since 2008, and that German industrial unions are still far more afraid of damage to German 'competitiveness' than of feeble domestic demand. In fact, there are passages in Blyth where the German aversion to inflation and indebtedness, described as belonging to a culture of 'First save, then buy' inaccessible to rational argument, ceases to look like a crazy idea and begins to appear as a rational expression of a structurally based interest: bad perhaps, but definitely not mad, considering how many German jobs depend on German export success. Viewed from that angle, the problem is not that the Germans don't know their macroeconomics. It is that thanks to the currency union, Germany is able to extend to the whole of Europe economic policies that may be right for itself but are dangerous for others.

It will be interesting to see how the German Left comes to terms with its new Keynesian champion. It is, after all, in full agreement with the SPD and the unions, just as with Merkel and the export industry, that it is vital to stick with the currency union as the supreme engine of the German export surplus, cost what it may. Here it definitively cannot call upon Blyth. His judgement on the currency union is simply devastating, and with good reason. For Blyth, the euro is a 'monetary doomsday device made by Europe for itself', and he repeatedly reminds his readers of Barry Eichengreen's insight, which goes back to Keynes himself, that in a democracy you cannot cling to a gold standard. If governments can neither inflate their way out of a crisis nor devalue their currency, all that remains is insolvency. This, however, would bring the banking system crashing down, and for that reason is impractical. That being so, the only remaining way out is internal devaluation achieved by reducing prices and wages, substituting for an external devaluation lowering the value of the national currency. 'This means austerity, which in turn means popular resistance. Sooner or later, then, either democracy will bring down the government, or the government will bring down democracy.'

Surprisingly, when Blyth reveals the superior ideas that are supposed to supersede austerity and misconceived interests, there is no further reference to the currency union, even though in his empirical case studies he repeatedly admits that austerity can lead to growth after all, albeit only in combination with the devaluation of the national currency. (Nor does he inquire whether his German Keynesian friends have ever taken steps to repeal the balanced budget amendment that was written into the German constitution under the European Monetary Union.) Instead, in the final chapter, we suddenly learn about problems with the national debt: previously a problem only for the banks and in the imagination of ordoliberal moralizers. But then, the solution, at least for Blyth, would not be so difficult. All that would be needed would be higher taxes on people with high incomes and great wealth in conjunction with 'financial repression': banks and insurance companies would have to be forced to invest in sovereign bonds at below-inflation interest rates and, assuming a more-or-less balanced budget thanks to the higher tax receipts, the debt mountain would soon melt away.

It may be assumed that Blyth regards the ECB's money-printing programme as a good idea, even though it is not clear whether the targeted 2 per cent inflation rate (which is hardly ambitious) can in fact be achieved. As for the taxation of high-income earners, Blyth seems greatly impressed by the stated intentions of the various governments. Can he really be as naïve about this as he pretends? Naturally, real growth would also be beneficial for debt reduction, but where will it come from, particularly if taxes are to rise? (And wasn't it Larry Summers himself, financial markets deregulator and 'Keynesian' all in one, who not too long ago thought it advisable to warn the world about a coming epoch of 'secular stagnation'?) Without inflation and growth not even a zero interest-rate policy will lead to debt reduction; just look at Japan. Apparently, however, even or precisely a confirmed Late Keynesian like Blythe seems inclined to avoid the question of whether an expansive fiscal and monetary policy can produce growth when all the players are up to their ears in debt. Nor does he wish to consider the fact that, well before the financial crash, debt both public and private had been rising steadily worldwide for decades, accompanied by falling, not rising, growth rates and – let us not forget – by increasing inequality of incomes and wealth.

In his polemic against the austerity fanatics, Blyth refers several times to the story of the drunk who looks for his car keys under a street lamp because that is the only place where he can see anything at all. Might the same parable not apply to people who for years now have viewed today's High Capitalism in the light of old Keynesian ideas, attempting to reinvigorate it with ever new cash injections? And this in spite of the experience of 2008 and the bubbles, always on the point of bursting, that are to be found on the edges of a growth path that benefits no more than a shrinking minority – a path that has for all others long since turned into a blind alley? If saving kills you, it doesn't necessarily follow that borrowing will restore your health.

CHAPTER 13

You Need a Gun

December 2017

WHAT IS THE RELATIONSHIP between coercion and consent? Under what circumstances does power turn into authority, brute force into legitimate leadership? Can coercion work without consent? Can consent be secured without coercion? Does political power depend on voluntary agreement and values shared in common, or does it grow out of the barrel of a gun? When ideas rule, how is that rule maintained? Can associations of equals – built on common interests, ideas and identities – endure, or must they degenerate into empires kept together by force? Such questions go to the foundations of political theory and practice. There is no better way to explore them than by tracing the complex career of the concept of hegemony, from the Greeks to today's 'international relations'. That is the task undertaken by Perry Anderson in *The H-Word* and *The Antinomies of Antonio Gramsci.**

The two books are closely connected. *The H-Word* reconstructs the long history of the concept of hegemony in twelve chapters,

---

* Perry Anderson, *The H-Word: The Peripeteia of Hegemony* and *The Antinomies of Antonio Gramsci*, London and New York: Verso, 2017.

moving from Thucydides via Lenin and Gramsci to various German and other imperialists, and from there to British, American and French post-war international relations theory. It takes in American political science and US strategic doctrine; the political economy of the Thatcher years; the work of Ernesto Laclau and Giovanni Arrighi; and, after a particularly exciting treatment of Asia and China from the time before the Warring Kingdoms to Mao and Deng Xiaoping, ends with today's European Union. *Antinomies* deals with Gramsci alone; essentially it is a reprint of a long essay published in 1977 in *New Left Review*. Both books are remarkable examples of the deep, historically situated reading of complex texts. *Antinomies* contains a preface reflecting on the interval since the first publication of the essay forty years ago, and in an appendix a fascinating report from 1933 on Gramsci in prison, written for the leadership of the Partito Comunista Italiano (PCI) by a fellow prisoner, published in English here for the first time.

The concept of hegemony has been and is still applied to relations between and within societies, to international politics as well as to national class struggle. Wherever they crop up, hegemons and their ideologues will do what they can to identify hegemony with legitimate authority: a social contract among equals in which leaders govern by consent and their followers give that consent in grateful return for services rendered. Yet when push comes to shove, as it very often does, the indispensable element of coercion in hegemony comes to the fore. Hegemony has never been sustained without coercion, but has more often than not been secured without consent. Hegemons don't always carry guns, but you can't be an effective hegemon without a decent supply of them. The purpose of hegemonic ideology is to make people believe that the hegemon is benevolent: having been granted power, the hegemon will act on behalf of those who cannot help themselves, whatever the cost to the hegemon. In compensation, the hegemon expects to be loved. But if it is to be secure when the moment of truth arrives, the hegemon must be able to instil fear. *Pace* Weber, a political regime is not stabilized by legitimacy, but by the capacity to substitute for it with coercion.

So far, so Machiavellian ('Is it better to be loved than feared or better to be feared than loved? One would of course like to be both; but it is difficult . . . and when a choice has to be made it is safer to be feared'). Anderson dispenses, one after another, with preachers of the 'white man's burden' school of belief in benevolent empire, among them Robert Keohane and Joseph Nye, with their self-serving fairy tales about a post-Vietnam US internationalism organized around 'complexity', 'interdependence', 'regime theory' and 'liberal institutionalism'. But his main focus is Gramsci, who as general secretary of the PCI was interned by Mussolini in 1926 and died in prison eleven years later. Gramsci had spent time in Moscow in the years after the Russian Revolution, and had been privy to the deadly serious strategic debates of the Third International. None of what he heard would, in his view, be helpful in leading the Italian party to victory. Italy was a deeply traditionalist European country, in which the dominance of capital was based on more than just brute force. It was deeply ingrained in 'civil society' and everyday life: the Church, the peasantry, small business, the urban bourgeoisie and parts of the intellectual and cultural elites were all more or less in the bourgeois-capitalist camp.

The concept of hegemony, as developed by Gramsci in his *Prison Notebooks*, had to be useful not only as an analytic tool, but also strategically: it must help not only to theorize the rule of capital, but to end it. Revolutionary action, in Gramsci's view, could succeed only once the social consent that gave capitalism its hegemony had been sufficiently undermined. The overthrow of capitalism must be preceded by cultural struggle, the changing of social life from the bottom up by replacing its bourgeois government and ideology with forms of collective solidarity and democratic self-organization. The problem of hegemony posed itself also within the anti-capitalist camp. The party of the working class would need to build alliances with other classes, which must be won over – through education, cooperation and organization – if they were to accept Communist Party leadership when the time came to dismantle the capitalist order.

Anderson's reading of Gramsci focuses on the practical problems he faced as he developed his perspective on the proletarian revolution. It wasn't just that Moscow might disapprove of his thinking but, perhaps more important, that his conceptualization of hegemony might suggest to PCI members that capitalism could be defeated by cultural struggle alone, making revolutionary violence unnecessary. Too much theoretical attention to civil society risked overlooking the state, and excessive concern with the element of consent in hegemony might underplay the role of coercion, which would be brought to bear by the state in the moment of truth, but also by the revolutionary party in defeating the state and, for a transitional period after victory, to keep its allies and former enemies in line.

The central question for Anderson is whether Gramsci, by assigning such a prominent place to the notion of hegemony in his reflections on revolutionary strategy, crossed the line into liberal reformism, or at least paved the way for it. Anderson thinks he did neither, emphatically defending Gramsci the revolutionary against those who, in the 1970s, exploited the *Prison Notebooks* to justify Eurocommunism's opportunistic switch from a revolutionary to a parliamentary path to socialism, or what they understood that to be. Anderson believes that the reformist tint of some passages in the *Notebooks* is owed to Gramsci's need to fool the fascist censors, who apparently collected his manuscripts each day for inspection. (It should also be borne in mind that the *Notebooks* were, after all, no more than notes for future elaboration.) Be that as it may, it is in the context of the turbulent 1970s – 'a time when there had recently been the largest mass strike in history in France, the overthrow of a government by workers in Britain, continuous outbreaks of revolt in Italy, the defeat of the United States in Vietnam, and a revolution in Portugal' – that Anderson's account of Gramsci must be read. At that time the Leninist tradition of discussing revolutionary strategy under advanced capitalism still made sense to some.

Anderson realizes that the time has passed for debating the amount of violence required for revolution, or the precise character of the proletarian dictatorship. But Gramsci remains relevant in helping us to understand how the apparently unforced consent to the regime of contemporary, intensified capitalism comes about, and where coercion may be at work in the operation of today's liberal democracies. In his preface to *Antinomies*, Anderson gives a deeply melancholic account of the new historical epoch that began when the revolutionary, or pseudo-revolutionary, surge of the 1970s ended with the terrorist spectacles staged by the likes of Baader-Meinhof and the Red Brigades – a new epoch that could dispense with ideology since capitalist hegemony now 'lay in a set of lifestyles, conducts, needs, demands, whose origin and end was in the world of commodities'. Now, he writes, there was 'no ethos, no directive idea, no concern with the inner life of the individual, which was delivered over to the market and the unconscious', and no need either for intellectuals and their passionate devotion to ideas. The new era's 'basic value' was 'tolerance, that is, indifference'. Still living in a 'relatively backward capitalist society' – one could describe it, alternatively, as a European society with strong precapitalist social bonds – Gramsci, according to Anderson, was unable to imagine that there could be a hegemony without hegemonic ideas, and indeed a hegemony 'that would rival in strength that of any in history' because it was 'anthropological, not ideological'.

What about coercion? Where is it at work in an individualistic consumer capitalist democracy in which dollars and votes aggregate freely to determine the optimal allocation of economic resources and political power? Marx's passage on 'primitive accumulation' in *Capital* comes to mind:

the advance of the capitalist mode of production develops a working class, which by education, tradition, habit, looks upon the conditions of that mode of production as self-evident laws of Nature. The organisation of the capitalist mode of production, once fully developed, breaks down all resistance . . . The dull compulsion of economic relations completes the subjection of the labourer to the capitalist. Direct force, outside economic conditions, is of course still used, but only exceptionally.

Replace 'labourer' with 'consumer' and note that, like the manufacture of consent, the production of compliance through coercion can proceed invisibly if it is embedded in the taken-for-granted structures of everyday life. That isn't to say that there is not, in this new society, a huge machinery of coercion, easily the largest and most expensive in history, maintained in readiness for the state of emergency that may one day have to be called: indelible records of each and every individual's plane journeys, bank card transactions, email, Facebook posts and so on, produced through a round-the-clock surveillance operation conducted by opaque bureaucracies, national and international, bigger than ever and still growing, not least under the cover of the 'war on terror', waged to enable the masses to continue living their pressured lives of competitive production and consumption.

Another testing ground for the continuing usefulness of the concept of hegemony is 'Europe', the political organization of a continent whose borders have only ever been vaguely defined. Is Germany the emerging hegemon of the European Union, this complex league of formally independent states: a Germany traditionally unwilling to play that role but now increasingly warming to it, even developing a sense of entitlement to it? What must be understood is that the business of post-heroic German society is business, not physical violence. It is true that Germany has recently become less pacifist: marginal participation in the illegal bombing of Serbia in 1999; a small detachment of troops in Afghanistan at the request of the US; air reconnaissance in Syria, to please Obama; minor military interventions in French Africa, in tribute to Franco-German friendship; an unknown number of special ops forces doing active duty in unknown places, together with colleagues from Denmark, Norway, Sweden and elsewhere, but always under US direction. Add the (generous) provision of airbases for the use of the US military and espionage facilities for the American 'intelligence community', as well as the half-price sale of submarines to Israel, and that's basically it – and there is unlikely to be much more for the foreseeable future. Casualties, not just on the German side, are unacceptable to the German public, so German commanders and their units wherever possible leave the killing (and the being killed) to the locals and the Americans.

How can such a country, voluntarily incapacitated and weaned off the sovereign use of military violence, to the satisfaction of its allies, be considered hegemonic? Perhaps only if we allow that economic coercion can take the place of physical coercion. Germany's most potent weapon in the European arena isn't a nuclear missile, but a hard currency. The prospect of the Bundeswehr invading Italy or France is unimaginable, but the Bundesbank may be seen as having done so in the past, and today the European Central Bank, acting together with the Eurogroup on German orders, may be in the process of creating an international regime.

It's as well to recall that the Economic and Monetary Union (EMU) was forced on Germany by its partners, France in particular; Germany resisted because, as its monetary 'realists' rightly predicted, assuming the role of hegemon would incur demands for redistributive benevolence. The story is complicated, but less so in the light of two often under-examined aspects of hegemony (they aren't overlooked by Anderson). First, the desire on the part of hegemons that their allies-turned-dependants organize themselves internally on the model of the hegemon – something that began with ancient Greece and didn't end with the American empire of the twentieth century. Second, that national and international struggles for hegemony should be considered together as interacting arenas in a multi-level power game. So, why did France (and Italy) force the role of European hegemon on an unwilling Germany? Because, in short, the French and Italian modernizing elites, in pursuit of domestic hegemony, were eager to force the hard German currency onto their own soft societies in order to make them fit for modern capitalism. Germans liked the idea in so far as it eliminated devaluation in other countries as a weapon of last resort against German competitiveness (devaluation being, in the German mindset, tantamount to cheating honest, hard-working, hard-saving German workers and employers). But there were also fears that Germany's new comrades-in-hard-money might not be up to the task of reforming their obstinate citizens, and that they would come looking for help in the form of a 'transfer union'.

Looking back, we can see now that the EMU and the divisions it causes in Europe are the result of historical miscalculations in the 1990s by Germany under Helmut Kohl and France under François Mitterrand. Kohl wanted political union to precede monetary union, which would effectively have eliminated Germany as a nation-state together with all other European nation-states. Kohl's imagined union would have been economically semi-sovereign on the model of the old Federal Republic, its central bank a replica of the Bundesbank. Mitterrand, by contrast, never once entertained the thought of letting France be subsumed into some multinational European state; he was too much of a Gaullist, or simply too French. What he had in mind wasn't political union but the economic reinvigoration of his own country through the introduction of a German-style European currency, by means of which France would itself rise to become the European hegemon – over Germany in particular – with enhanced, nuclear-powered national sovereignty and, one may assume, a (European) central bank more supportive of public deficits than the German version. Both projects failed dismally. Now Germany is working hard, with the help of co-operative national governments, to have its domestic political economy extended to Europe as a whole, the aim being to keep the euro while retaining, for free, the advantages conferred on Germany by its superior competitiveness. So far its efforts have been in vain. The French and Italian elites find themselves unable to force the blessings of neoliberalism on their countries, which now depend on German beneficence for their survival. The result is, *pace* Anderson, not hegemony but a profound political deadlock that nobody knows how to resolve.

It is true, though, that underneath the European stalemate a strange kind of hegemonic consciousness without hegemony is developing in Germany. Armed with 'values' in place of guns, a broad German mainstream feels entitled to tell other Europeans, in the name of European unity, what they must aim to become – which is to say, more like the German mainstream. Consent is demanded on moral grounds, and refusal is met with sad disappointment. Central to this is an appeal to a version of universalism that denies nations the right to exist in their own way, indeed to exist as nations at all. There is some resemblance here to US liberal interventionism, although in the German case the means are restricted to moral admonition and, increasingly, the threat to halt European Union subsidies if countries do not live up to universal – that is, German – standards: Hungary and Poland, for example, with respect to immigration.

The German idea, if there is one, is European hegemony as leadership, based not on coercion but on moral superiority – a utopia which, as Anderson makes clear, cannot work, either within nations or between them. Indeed, as seen from Berlin, Europe is far from being a well-ordered league of states ready to follow a German example. Keeping the likes of Macron in power by means of quiet economic support was not made any easier by the results of the recent German election: there are now parties in the Bundestag that won't be shy about asking impolite questions. Brexit will make things even more difficult. While Merkel's instinct is to want a reversal of the UK referendum result, France is happy to be rid of the British, and sooner rather than later. The French will use the opportunity to pursue once again 'ever closer union among the peoples of Europe', hoping to consolidate a Mediterranean coalition that will keep Germany in its place. As a counterweight to the Southern member states, Germany needs the Eastern ones, which means maintaining a moderate level of tension with Russia. This, in turn, requires American backing, in case the going gets tough. Yet Germany also needs Russian energy, to a degree that the nuclear-powered French do not, and it needs the Eastern Europeans to accept their share of migrants – for which they will need to be paid off with German taxpayers' money. Meanwhile, at home, any German government will have to pay tribute, symbolic and material, to the eurozealots in the media, and among the Greens and Social Democrats, who continue to clamour for 'European integration': for a union without hegemony and its discontents, based solely on 'European values' and on publicly expressed disgust with Trump, Putin and Erdoğan. Not easy, to say the least.

CHAPTER 14

What about Capitalism?

June 2017

THE BOOK TO BE reviewed here – *The Lure of Technocracy* – is Jürgen Habermas's latest statement on Europe, its crisis, its politics and its prospects.* It is the English translation – a remarkably good one – of *Im Sog der Technokratie*. The German original came out as Volume XII of *Kleine politische Schriften*, a series that dates back to 1980 and with which, according to Habermas, it is to conclude. The twelve volumes, all of them collections of occasional papers, interviews and public lectures produced alongside Habermas's main works, have long become an object of wide admiration, in Germany and beyond, for their unique combination of political activism, profound scholarship and, not least, brilliant essayistic prose, and they can already now claim a prominent place in the political and cultural history of post-war Germany. *The Lure of Technocracy* consists of ten pieces from the last three or four years, seven of them more or less directly concerned with European integration and its crisis since 2008.†

---

* Jürgen Habermas, *The Lure of Technocracy*, trans. Ciaran Cronin, Cambridge: Polity, 2015.

† The last chapter in this sequence, chapter 7, is a review of a book published by

The three remaining chapters, assembled under the title *German Jews, Germans and Jews,* are indispensable reading for anyone interested in West German intellectual life after 1945. Although they stand for an important subtheme of Habermas's Europeanism, I will focus on the seven chapters that precede them.

Habermas's European writings are inextricably linked into his sociological and philosophical scholarship as it has developed since the 1960s. One may even go as far as to say that how 'Europe' will fare will be a test of whether or not Habermasian general theory of human and moral evolution actually 'works'. Indeed Habermas, one of the foremost public intellectuals in Europe and beyond, may have become as active a political agent as he is in the battles over the future constitution of Europe precisely because his stake in their outcome is so high. A book review, short as it must be, cannot possibly pursue the manifold theoretical ramifications that inform a political vision as carefully calibrated as this one to fit an immensely ambitious general perspective on history and society. On the other hand, criticizing Habermas simply on empirical grounds is not enough, if only because his work is not just about the factual but also, and most importantly, about the presumably possible – placing the critic at risk of appearing as a petty priest of a dogmatic cult of the superficially real assaulting a prophet of a higher truth.

The Lure of Technocracy may legitimately be read as a summary of long years of scholarly reflection and public intervention on its subject, indicating where the theoretical-political project it represents – a project occasionally called upon by the Brussels Eurocracy for ideological legitimation purposes – has today arrived. Looked

---

this author in 2013. The review is unenthusiastic enough in parts for it to be included in the following discussion. For an extensive response to it, see Streeck, 'Vom DM-Nationalismus zum Euro-Patriotismus? Eine Replik auf Jürgen Habermas', *Blätter für deutsche und internationale Politik,* vol. 58, no. 9, 2013, pp. 75–92. English trans.: 'Small-State Nostalgia? The Currency Union, Germany, and Europe: A Reply to Jürgen Habermas', *Constellations,* vol. 21, no. 2, 2014, pp. 213–21.

at this way, however, the book gives its readers reasons for concern. To begin with, its chapters never discuss the nature of the economic interests and conflicts underlying the contemporary politics of Europe and European integration – suggesting, as though this was still the social democratic 1980s or the Third Way 1990s, that a future European democracy enshrined in a European constitution will as a matter of course come with a primacy of European politics over European and, indeed, global capitalism. The book also misconceives the role of the European Monetary Union, present-ing it as promoting European unity-cum-democracy, while in fact it divides Europe into hostile national camps by forcing its nations under a uniform monetary regime that suits only some of them, especially Germany, at the expense of others. Moreover, it not only entertains a technocratic conception of the way to European democracy, but also remains strangely vague on how a democratic Europe, reformed according to Habermasian princi-ples on the foundations of the European Union of today, would differ from the present technocratic one.

Furthermore, the book also leaves more questions open than it answers on the status of European nations in a united democratic Europe and on the nature of the future democratic European entity, except that it rules out a supranational state[*] – even though at the same time, remarkably, it expects a *democratically united non-state Europe* to perform core state functions, like European

---

[*]   Of course this has for several years now been the official Brussels position, where the would-be rulers of the 'ever closer union of the European peoples', while refusing to take part in the building controversy over what is the *finalité* of European integration, strictly deny that what they have in mind is a 'United States of Europe'. Obviously this is to pacify the citizens of member countries who in their vast majority find this prospect horrifying. Perhaps Habermas's renunciation of a state-building project may also be political rhetoric to mislead the uninitiated. In this case, however, one wonders if he has understood the other function of the recent anti-statism of Brussels, which is to reassure international capital that the new European entity will not undertake to domesticate it in the way the nation-state has tried to and may still return to trying.

'self-assertion' in global politics and imposing 'social justice' on the capitalist European economy. Moreover, it avoids the issue, central for Habermas's theory of an evolving moral universalism, of whether the future European construction will be distinctly European or, alternatively, anticipatorily cosmopolitan – in other words, whether united Europe will have a substantively fixed or a contingently moving border. It in addition assigns to Germany of all countries a leading role in the democratic denationalization of Europe, a role it is to seek in order to protect itself and the world from a return of imperial 'power fantasies' by dissolving as a nation into an encompassing denationalized Europe. Among other things, this overlooks that the same monetary union which Habermas considers an indispensable stepping stone towards that Europa has already turned the Euroland economy into an extension of the German economy, under a really existing German hegemony dedicated to, of all things, spreading ordoliberal 'reform' to the rest of Europe, to the considerable annoyance of some, if not all, of Germany's partners.

This being so, it cannot come as a surprise that nothing in Habermas's book prepares the reader for the powerful popular reaction currently observed in Europe to the wilful destruction of national sovereignty, national democracy and the national welfare state on which 'the European project' has in the past two decades embarked, in faithful execution of the functional imperatives of neoliberalizing global capitalism. In Habermas's world, the only possible explanation for today's escalating crisis of European integration is cognitive and moral deficits on the part of both governments and the governed, while the only solution are stronger 'pro-European' leaders, wherever they may come from (Germany?), ready to stick 'more Europe' to the reluctant masses. That this might end up producing even more anti-Europe – something that a growing number of observers, surely not all of them 'nostalgic fools', have for some time seen coming – is never even considered. Sadly enough, years of debate over the evolving empirical observables in Europe and the theories needed to make sense of them have had no impact on a political imaginary which, after all, must conceive of itself as dedicated to principles of discursive rationality.

The blind spots in Habermas's anti-national Europeanism are interestingly linked to his system: theoretically neutered concept of capitalism. Having at some point in the evolution of his social theory granted immunity to a 'globalized' capitalist economy by redefining the interests vested in it into 'problems' calling for technically correct 'solutions', Habermas can treat really existing politics – the rough and tumble of local, regional, national collective interests, histories, languages, experiences, identities, hostilities, cultures, idiosyncrasies and passions – as non-substantial illegitimate impediments on the way to *democracy as it should be*: universalistic, dispassionate, global, deliberative, cooperative, and apparently without any need to override obstinate interests in the unlimited accumulation of capital by use of collectively mobilized power and legitimate force (that is, of the very state capacity that Habermas, for whatever reason, denies his European democracy). What remains at the end are normative prescriptions of rational-cum-moral cosmopolitan political conduct for which there is no real world out there that could live by them. One must be afraid that all a theory of this sort can do is move the theorist into a position of moral superiority in relation to a political reality that has no chance but being found guilty of failing to verify theoretical predictions that are in fact moral commands.

Among the puzzles in Habermas's writings on 'Europe' is that he never cares to explain why he insists on identifying the prospect of European democracy with, of all things, the Economic and Monetary Union: from the beginning a profoundly compromised monetary regime that has in the few years of its existence critically divided Europe instead of uniting it.* In this, strangely enough, Habermas takes sides with none other than Angela Merkel and her frivolous claim that 'if the euro fails, Europe fails'† – identifying a 2,000-year-old cultural and political landscape of grand and jointly produced diversity with a trivial utilitarian construction that happens to serve above all the interests of the German export industries.‡ He does not discuss why *bona fide* European countries such as Denmark, Sweden, Norway, the United Kingdom (whose language we speak when we act as 'Europeans') and Switzerland have refrained from joining EMU, not to mention acknowledgement of the fact that after the Euroland experience they will not in any foreseeable future apply for membership (and neither will Poland, Hungary, the Czech Republic, etc.) – provided the less-than-fully-common currency will survive the next decade, which is far from certain. *Euroland is not Europe, and never will be*, even if the euro is here to stay, Habermas and Merkel notwithstanding. Moreover, in addition to dividing Europe into Euroland and

---

* Wolfgang Streeck, 'Why the Euro Divides Europe', *New Left Review*, no. 95, 2015, pp. 5–26.

† Even though he is very well aware of all or most of the problems of the EMU.

‡ In the only place where Habermas discusses this – in an interview with an Austrian weekly newspaper – he refers to his personal 'knowledge of history and the political life experience of a German of my generation' to argue that 'it would be demoralizing if the currency union were to fail for clear reasons of national egoism' – which, the context suggests, means that the euro would fail, if it did, because of *German* national egoism, making it a German responsibility not to be 'egoistic' for the sake of European unity. That the euro might fail because it would turn out to be an economic disaster for some of its member states while being a boon for others is not taken into consideration since, presumably, whatever economic problems it might produce could be cured by German altruism motivated by the haunting memories of the German past. Habermas also predicts that a 'failure' of the euro 'would provide the starting signal for the right-wing populism that has undergone a revival in all of our countries'. This misrepresents the causal relationship as it was and is the defence of the euro that gave the 'starting signal' for 'anti-European', sovereigntist movements in several countries, where it was not least fear of German hegemony that led to popular demands, for example, in France, for the euro to be rescinded rather than saved.

non-Euroland, the euro has divided Euroland itself into debtor and creditor countries, allocating to Germany in particular the role of despised economic taskmaster,* while furthermore dividing member countries internally into 'pro-European' and 'anti-European' camps, the latter rapidly increasing in strength, especially where they are of a right-wing nationalist sort.

Why does Europe, or better, the Europe of Habermasian theory, need the euro? Here Habermas, remarkably, comes out as an unabashed functionalist. Several times he refers to the common currency as a 'cunning of economic reason' with respect to the Europeanization-through-denationalization of Europe – an institutional constraint that, once instituted, will, at the penalty of severe economic losses, force European countries to advance towards political, that is, economic, fiscal and social policy union, and to democratic union to boot, even if their citizens object to it. Since abandoning the euro would remove that constraint and leave European integration without what Habermas sees as its unification engine, it must not even be considered, and any 'talk of a plan B', for example, in relation to the Greek calamities, must be discredited, if necessary morally. Obviously, what is lurking in the background of this is the so-called 'neofunctionalist' theory of European integration as developed by the German-American political scientist Ernst Haas out of long conversations with Jean Monnet, one of the engineers of post-war integrated Western Europe.† Its key concept is that of 'spillover', meaning the horizontal spread – at the time, of course, in no more than six countries! – of unified European institutions from sector to sector, driven by and compensating for the lack of a supra-nationally minded citizenry.

---

* A sort of leadership it has now sought and found also in a second field, that of humanitarian charity, by masterminding the European 'refugee crisis'.

† E.B. Haas, *The Uniting of Europe*, Stanford, CA: Stanford University Press, 1958.

Of course, the problem with neofunctionalist integration theory is that it is profoundly technocratic, which is not surprising considering that it was inspired by someone like Monnet, a French technocrat who oversaw the early phase of European integration, in particular the European Community for Coal and Steel. For some time now it has dawned on most political scientists working on the subject that the era of neofunctionalism is over. As integration penetrates deeper and deeper into the fabric of national societies, spillover can no longer be counted on to move integration forwards. Neofunctionalism, we now know, worked only under the 'permissive consensus' of the founding years, when nobody really cared what European elites were doing 'in Europe'. But as integration progressed and as a result became politicized, further progress came to require more than technocratic 'necessity': not the behind-the-back functionalist reason of the economically inevitable, but political reason.

Here nations come in, and with them Habermas's stubborn denial of their factual existence as moral and economic communities of shared understandings and institutionalized solidarity, or in any case of their moral right to exist as such. Completely in accord with the eurocrats, Habermas finds nations embarrassing, presumably not just for political reasons but also because they do not fit his theory of modernity, and he wants them to go away because they might obstruct what he hopes will be the unstoppable progress of economic 'globalization' promoting moral cosmopolitanism. Where one might have expected a serious discussion of the relationship between national and supranational politics in Europe on the one hand and the domestication versus the liberalization of European capitalism on the other, yielding a fourfold table as sociologists have been used to since the days of Talcott Parsons, all one finds is unconditional partisanship for the non-national and supranational. Here Habermas does not refrain from aggressive polemics aimed at excluding those unwilling to subscribe to his views from the spectrum of legitimate opinion, as in a manifesto titled *Wählt Europa!* (Elect Europe!) issued in the run-up to the 2014 European Parliament elections by the late Ulrich Beck, with Habermas its first signatory, which warned against an 'anti-European revolution of the right and the left Right' (in German: *eine anti-europäische Revolution der rechten und linken Rechten*). But morally disparaging national communitarian institutions and solidarities in the name of an under-socialized cosmopolitanism, and one disarmed in its relationship with capitalism by a refusal to assume the tasks and the burdens of a state, is dangerous. The repressed may powerfully return, and then in the distorted shape of a Marine Le Pen and consorts: of nationalist movements that will not confine themselves to insisting on sovereign powers to deal with their problems on their own responsibility, but combining this with hatred of anyone they care to define as not belonging to their kind. I am afraid that Habermas and his opportunistic friends in Brussels and Berlin will to the very end and beyond refuse to understand that their brand of Europeanism was, and is, a potent cause of the hostile parochialism that is so frighteningly proliferating even in the most liberal and internationalized countries of Europe.

Not only may the cunning of economic reason fail to do its job, due to stubborn refusal on the part of citizens to see the light and say B after their governors have said A on their behalf. I leave aside for the moment the question whether Habermas would consider such resistance to technocracy democratic. More important at this point, Habermas never doubts that imposing a common monetary regime on countries with different political economies and social structures does in fact reflect 'economic reason', not to mention asking whose reason it reflects. For Habermas, money is money, and all that matters is its territorial domain, the bigger, the more universalistic, the better. Extension of a legal tender's jurisdiction in the name of 'economic reason' is assumed to be so all-round beneficial that on its coattails a coterminous extension of political jurisdiction – a departure from *Kleinstaaterei* towards, apparently, something like *Großstaaterei* – must inexorably follow, 'nostalgic' resistance from the uninitiated being nothing but 'foolish'. Comparison between the suffering of the Mediterranean countries inside Euroland and the prosperity of the Danish, Swedish, Norwegian and Icelandic economies – countries that have chosen to remain free to use monetary policy in the service of their respective niche strategies for the global economy* – is not admitted into evidence. This is probably because it might suggest that less economic universalism matching the constitutive particularism of really existing human societies might be a more democratic answer to our current political-economic predicaments than more political universalism trying to match the infinite universalistic advance of money and markets – the latter for Habermas apparently the predetermined course of historical evolution, normatively desirable and technically necessary at the same time.

Habermas's confidence in the cunning of technocratic reason replacing national particularism with European universalism raises the question of what exactly the fault is that he finds with the really existing European technocracy, and what he hopes will take its place when its 'lure' – or, perhaps, its cunning? – will have done its work. But at this point, again, the argument remains hazy, although what is at issue would appear to be nothing less than the difference between capitalism as it is now and capitalism contained and constrained by democratic social and political powers. Instead, Habermas speaks of a 'transfer union', without discussing who is to transfer what, and how much, and to whom. More generally, he observes that a

> technocracy without democratic roots would neither have the power nor the motivation to accord sufficient weight to the

---

* Note that Iceland, while hit hardest by the financial crisis, was able, having kept its own currency, to devise probably the most socially compatible solution to it, as even the International Monetary Fund has admitted. Consider also the United Kingdom, where monetary sovereignty helped the country avoid what would otherwise have been an even more severe crisis.

demands of the electorate for social justice, status security, public services and collective goods, in the event of a conflict with the systemic demands for competitiveness and economic growth.

But would a technocracy *with* democratic roots? Habermas seems to believe that the political-economic problem of Europe is basically a lack of sensitivity to popular demands in European decision-making centres that could in principle easily be remedied if only such demands were given a constitutional opportunity to make themselves heard, for which a parliament devoid of a state would suffice. Moving electoral democracy from the national level, where rising interdependence has rendered it ineffective, to the European supranational level would, or so Habermas suggests, make 'systemic demands' once again malleable to human counter-demands, simply by enlarging 'the basis of legitimation' to match 'the expansion of steering capacities.'*

Is this in any way realistic? For Habermas, the enemy is not capitalism but technocracy, and only as long as its congenital insensitivity to popular sentiments endangers the project of European denationalization. In this perspective, the transfer of political-economic decision-making in past decades to electorally unaccountable institutions, such as an independent central bank, appears as no more than a side-effect of honest efforts to resolve increasingly difficult problems of international interdependence. De-democratization did occur, but mostly by accident and oversight in the heat of a running battle with difficult problems of coordination, perhaps reinforced by deplorable although corrigible non-democratic habits on the part of hard-working problem-solvers, but clearly not with a pro-capitalist neoliberal intention or as a concession to growing capitalist power. Thus it

---

* Which would, according to Habermas, in a surprising adaptation of European technospeak, also 'promote growth and competitiveness in the Eurozone as a whole'.

can be healed, the 'systemic demands' of contemporary capitalism notwithstanding. Indeed ultimately, it is not capitalism that is the problem in Habermas's Europe, but its management. What is wrong with the Europe of monetary union, Habermas implies, is not that it is pro-capitalist, or subservient to capitalist interests, but that it is – contingently – non-democratic, thereby subverting the struggle against the real enemy: nationalism. Democracy can correct this by making the demands of ordinary people heard as decision-makers attend to 'systemic demands', refilling the system's supply of legitimacy. No need to confront the increasingly insatiable demands of the profit-dependent classes for precedence of their interests over those of the rest of society. In fact, class interests do not really appear in Habermasian European theory, only biased cognitions of decision-makers in need of democratic correction. This disregards the fundamental insight of critical political economy that 'the economy' is not about more or less enlightened management but about more or less manifest class conflict, in which the adversary of 'the people' is not technocracy but capital.* Hidden behind what dresses up as systemic necessities, indeed as 'economic laws' and 'economic reason', are interests as shaped by evolving relations of economic and political power, today in particular the changing power balance between increasingly global capital and inevitably local labour. There is no way one can talk about European democracy without also talking about capitalism.

---

* Chantal Mouffe, *On the Political*, London: Routledge, 2005.

CHAPTER 15

Two Worlds, Not One

November 2018

For a social scientist, reading Darwin's *Origin of Species* (from here on *Origin*)* is a simultaneously humbling and reassuring experience. What an achievement! Science and scientific writing at their best. A book that is the product of long thinking, such as we, haunted by deadlines, can today only dream of, and written in a clear, engaging language, immensely readable for even the (educated and interested) layperson. Everything is as simple as possible but no simpler, as allegedly demanded by none less than Albert Einstein himself. And profoundly honest: the open questions, the remaining mysteries carefully exposed, careful attention paid to the difficult spots, and the arguments of the opposition, both real and anticipated, treated with polite respect.

What can be reassuring here if we know all too well that we will most likely never match this unmatchable masterpiece? Social scientists are too often afflicted by what has been called 'physics

---

* Shorthand for the title of the first edition, *On the Origin of Species by Means of Natural Selection: or, The Preservation of Favoured Races in the Struggle for Life*. Quotes are from Darwin, *The Origin of Species*, London: CRW, 2004 [1859].

envy' – a sense of inferiority over their theories' inability to predict the future. Does what they have to offer really deserve to be called theory? While most physicists do not waste their time arguing with social scientists about whether what they are doing is 'theory' or even 'science', it is economists – the modern, mainstream ones who insist that they are anything but social scientists – who keep claiming that a theory that fails to yield predictions cannot qualify as one. Their theory, of course, predicts, if only in principle (principle aside, its predictions, although hawked with unlimited scientistic self-confidence, normally turn out to be wrong, especially in times when true predictions would be particularly welcome). It takes a theory to beat a theory, economists keep telling social scientists. By 'theory' they mean a Newtonian theory, like theirs, one that presupposes a Newtonian universe: naturally in equilibrium, governed by universal laws of motion, by constant forces like gravity that direct any movement of any object towards a predetermined, and therefore predictable, position, under an unchanging and unchangeable, clockwork-like natural order.*

Taking a fresh look at *Origin* seems like the ideal treatment for social scientists suffering from the physics envy instilled by their colleagues from the economics department. Darwin's is clearly a theory: it subsumes a vast number of disparate facts under beautifully simple general principles that remain resolutely open to being challenged by empirical evidence. But equally clearly, it is not a Newtonian theory, as it neither aims at nor claims to be capable of

---

* Remember that Adam Smith's favourite scientific discipline was Newtonian astronomy. Whether 'the economy' is in fact a Newtonian universe cannot be a concern for an economic 'science' that can regard itself as science only by attributing to its object world the properties it assumes are required for a truly scientific theory. To the extent that its world fails to display those properties, economic science will squeeze it into the Procrustean bed of its requisite ontology, regardless how much it hurts. In case 'the economy' cannot be shown to be in equilibrium, a better theory is sought that can do the trick. Alternatively, an economy out of equilibrium can be argued to be on its way back to one; or contingent disequilibrium can be attributed to human meddling insufficiently informed by economic science.

prediction. Instead it is a historical theory: it undertakes to explain how the real world as it exists today has come to be what it is, without predicting what it will be like next. *Origin* is living proof that a theory that explains the present by its past while leaving the future open can be a respectable, 'scientific', bona fide theory – even though it is a historical one that depends on 'storytelling', just as is social science, which is precisely for this reason considered by many, even some of its producers, as lacking in scientific dignity.

What can Darwinian evolutionary biology, as developed in *Origin*, contribute to a social science no longer willing to deprive its object world of its historicity? In what sense can social science be encouraged by a close reading of biological Darwinism to cease being ashamed of itself and give up whatever Newtonian pretensions it may have adopted under pressure from a de-socialized economics? And what, if anything, can social science learn from its homologies with Darwinian natural history? Compared to the divine clockwork of Newtonian physics, there are intriguing ontological similarities between Darwinian evolutionary biology and a non-Newtonian social science that strongly suggest the possibility of concepts from the former inspiring empirical and theoretical progress in the latter. Just as in the social world, the world of living organisms as depicted in *Origin* is beset by an *intrinsic restlessness* that is a source of permanent instability and continuous change. Both biological and social life appear *inherently creative* – which is another way of saying that they are *historical*, which in turn implies that their emerging future is always an open one. Social theory, this suggests, can rely on evolutionary biology at least to reassure itself that it is not its fault if its objects, as it represents them, appear noisy, fuzzy, restive, eventful, transitory, temporary, surprising and always more or less out of balance – and that there is no need for a theory of society to take their life out of them for social science to become possible.

There is no ambiguity in *Origin* as to where the restlessness of life on earth is rooted. Life, like history, is all about reproduction. Reproduction is by descent: earlier generations are followed by later ones, in unending sequence, from the past to the present, and from there into the future. Reproduction by descent means renewal, in the sense of continuity and change at the same time, as descent is always *with modification*. Darwin didn't know what exactly caused that modification – genetic mutation was not yet known in his time. But empirical observation had convinced him that reproduction was never perfect and inevitably came with variation. Moreover, such variation seemed to him not directional or directed, not aimed at any particular end – in other words, not teleological – but accidental, randomly deviating from parent organisms and randomly distributed among their offspring.

Reproductive variation, then, operates like, in modern language, a stochastic source. But this does not make natural history chaotic. Variation from parent to offspring and between offspring, while random, is always gradual and typically minute. *Natura non facit saltus* (Nature does not make leaps) is a time-honoured principle of European scientific reason that goes back to Aristotle, one to which Darwin at strategic turns in his argument pledges his firm allegiance. Moreover, to account for the structuring – the orderliness – of natural history, *descent with modification* is complemented by two other key concepts of Darwinian theory, the *struggle for existence* and *natural selection*. Drawing on Malthus, Darwin posits that reproduction increases the number of organisms geometrically, outpacing any possible linear increase in the resources needed to sustain them. All living organisms, therefore, have to *struggle* for their survival with other living organisms, of the same or of different species, in what Darwin refers to as *the economy of nature*. Survival allows for and indeed consists in reproduction; death means exclusion from it. Which organisms survive the struggle depends on the endowment of physical properties and instinctive behaviours received, *with modification,* from progenitors; organisms that fit the current conditions of the struggle for existence better can reproduce while the others remain unselected by Nature* and are expelled from natural history.

Natural history, then, proceeds through minimal differences generated by chance and through the favours bestowed by the external, 'natural' conditions of their day on variants, or mutants, which happen to be better than their competition at coping with such conditions, including the presence of other classes of organisms equally subject to continuous change through natural selection. In selecting 'favoured races', 'Nature' is limited to what is supplied to it by what it has inherited, with modification, from previous generations. Nature, in other words, can work only with material that it has itself produced in the past, and the changes it can make on it can only be gradual and incremental. In improving its creatures, in the sense of adjusting them better to contingent circumstances, Nature must be content with small steps, as major change can come about only by continuous accumulation of minor changes over many generations, normally meaning very long periods of time. There is never a new beginning, no reset button, no revolution, just evolution. Even when a meteorite radically disrupts the external conditions of life, Nature must carry on with what the disaster has left, unable to go back to square one to start again with a radically new design of its productions.

Two Worlds, Not One

So again, what can a curious social scientist learn from one of the model achievements of the modern scientific tradition? It seems to me that above all we must not be misled, impressed by Darwin's stunning demonstration of the power of theory, to biologize human action and human society, thereby de-socializing it. We

---

* Where Darwin speaks of nature metaphorically as though it commanded an active capacity, he writes it with a capital letter. I follow this usage here where it suggests itself in paraphrasing Darwin.

must not reconceptualize the social world as another biological world, for example, by giving up the notion of meaning-oriented social action and replacing it with instinct-controlled behaviour, in the belief that the lesson to be learned from Darwin is that society must be naturalized to be accessible to evolutionary theory. Rather, the task is to apply evolutionary theory to *society as society*, as a world of its own that, while grown out of and still rooted in the biological world, can and should not be reduced to it. The idea is to transport Darwinian evolutionism into social theory, to help understand a subject matter – social action and social institutions – for which it was not conceived, without thereby buying into biologism, that is, disrespecting its particular nature. I suggest that this is both possible and far from dangerous to social science's theoretical and political health. In fact, I believe it can be extremely productive, not least in that it draws our attention to important *differences* between societal and natural history, and may even help us understand how society and biology, or humanity and nature, are related, not just systematically but also historically.

Social science, that is to say, should feel encouraged by the unquestionable scientific character of Darwinian evolutionism to do what it urgently should do; namely, to reintroduce history into social theory. Having worked as a social scientist on institutional change, I have become convinced that we need to restore history and historical development as central concepts of our discipline, or else we will forever be confined to a sterile, formalistic, essentially technocratic presentism that misses what is most important about society: its boundedness in time and space.* Of course we cannot and should not even try to revive the teleological

---

* It is in this context that I first hit on Darwinian evolutionism as a theoretical model, in an effort to revive the possibility of a historical theory of capitalist development by freeing it from teleological implications. An initial outline of the argument, with a section on evolution, is found in Streeck, 'Institutions in History: Bringing Capitalism Back In', in John Campbell et al., eds, *Handbook of Comparative Institutional Analysis*, Oxford: Oxford University Press, 2010, pp. 659–86.

determinism of the nineteenth century that informed sociological theory basically until the demise of modernization theory in the 1970s. But this does not dispense us from trying to understand the way history moves and is moved. It is from this perspective that I find Darwin's *Origin* so stimulating, as it offers a model of a theory of history as continuous, endogenous, self-driven incremental change regularly producing novel – in the sense of *a priori* unknowable – but never terminal, historical conditions, connecting novelty to continuity by emphasizing the gradual nature of change, that is, the dependence of the future on the present, and of the present on the past.

To realize the full benefits Darwinian evolutionism holds in store for it, I believe social science must distance itself from a number of previous attempts, some of them quite prominent, to apply evolutionary theory, or whatever they have taken it for, to society. Some of these build on the Darwinian 'struggle for existence' a Panglossian functionalism in which the empirical world is necessarily the best of all possible worlds, or would be if competitive 'natural selection' were not frivolously interfered with by scientifically uninformed do-gooders. Others draw on Darwin's treatment of the behavioural programmes of organisms as being in the same way subject to variation and natural selection as physical properties, in an attempt to justify a biologistic-reductionist conception of human nature and society that replaces action with behaviour and norms with instincts. None of this, I suggest, is justified, let alone required, by the Darwin of *Origin*. The former confuses relative with absolute 'perfection' of evolutionary outcomes, while the latter implies that the Darwinian combination of stochastic variation with systemic selection – which is what makes Darwinian evolutionism a theory of history with an open future – can be translated to social science only at the expense of adopting a biological-naturalistic, nonagentic definition of the human actor. I will briefly address both in turn.

Regarding organisms' functional perfection – the degree to which they are ideally adapted to the demands made of their 'struggle for existence' – Darwin leaves no doubt, where he addresses the issue systemically, that his world is a historical and not a functionalist one:

> As natural selection acts by competition, it adapts the inhabitants of each country only in relation to the degree of perfection of their associates . . . Nor ought we to marvel if all the contrivances in nature, be not, as far as we can judge, absolutely perfect; and if some of them be abhorrent to our idea of fitness . . . The wonder indeed is, on the theory of natural selection, that more cases of the want of absolute perfection have not been observed . . .*

Evolutionary fit is relative, not absolute – relative to location in time and space, to available biological material, and to environmental challenges. At the time an organism is observed, natural evolution may still be under way towards more 'perfect' adaptation; or what 'Nature' can do for it may be limited by its inherited properties; or what may have once been hard-gained 'optimal' adjustment may have been rendered useless by changes in the external circumstances of the 'struggle for life'. If external conditions are prone to change faster than the organisms struggling under them, perfect adaptation may indeed be no more than a moving target that is never fully reached – and if in exceptional cases it is, it may soon be undone by changed conditions in the organic or the inorganic world, or both.

---

* Darwin, *Origins*, p. 507. See also the example of the bug Darwin discovered on an island that contained almost no flying insects. Apparently its ancestors had been those mutants of a former species that were not very good at flying. The better fliers were regularly driven into the sea by the strong winds, and they became extinct. Fittest for the 'struggle for existence' were those individuals that were least fit for flying.

Assuming less-than-perfect adaptive fit to be normal undermines the functionalist logic of explanation to which both biology and economics incline. A functionalist explanation treats effect as cause, via 'backward induction', which makes for an unambiguous solution only if the effect is assumed to be perfect. Moreover, backward induction entails a temptation to redefine cause as intention, and indeed as strategically rational and empirically effective intention. This seems easier in social science, with human rather than nonhuman agents. Note, however, that social conditions can often be explained only as 'unintended consequences' of social action.* This, if functionalism is to remain functionalism, requires theory to specify mechanisms that ensure that those consequences, even though unintended, aggregate into the right, functionally desirable condition at the level of the society as a whole. In biology, complicated and often nonintuitive accounts of random variation and historical selection are simplified, for convenience or for the benefit of the nitwits,† by recourse to a language of strategic action attributing rational and strategically successful intentionality to organisms undergoing – or 'in pursuit of' – adaptive change. Projecting intentionality into the natural world is the reverse side of subjecting the social world to biological reductionism – fake intentionality dressing up cause as reason while biologism turns reason into instinct. The female peacock selects her mate on the basis of the beauty of his tail because she strategically understands that a beautiful tail signals strong genes that will improve the prospects of her offspring to survive – while the male poet writes his poems, not in order to make a living or symbolize an aesthetic experience, but to get as many admiring women as possible to let him fertilize their eggs.

---

* Robert K. Merton, *Social Theory and Social Structure*, Glencoe, IL: The Free Press, 1957.

† And generally to overcome the fundamental counter-intuitiveness of evolutionist explanations of extremely complex biological phenomena as results of chance – of apes randomly hitting the keys of typewriters – rather than rational design.

As to biological reductionism as such, it essentially assumes that human actors are endowed with hardwired behavioural dispositions 'selected' by 'evolution', dispositions that are single-mindedly focused on physical reproduction. All human action is assumed to be controlled by them, regardless of the meanings actors attribute to it. In this view of the world, human actors are typically victims of false consciousness: while they believe they are serving cultural values or fulfilling moral obligations, actually they are driven by instincts established during and inherited from natural history, whose true purpose may remain entirely unknown to them. Human action is effectively controlled by instincts such that it is 'rational' with respect to its 'real' function, which is to secure reproduction. Ultimately this makes access to reproduction the secret but decisive, and indeed the only 'real', ultimate motive driving agents and shaping their social relations. For example, a popular biologistic-reductionist evolutionary model of social action explains sexually unfaithful behaviour of human males in societies where faithfulness is a social value as an inherited 'rational' desire on their part to spread their genes to 'capture' as many eggs as possible. Female faithfulness, in turn, is explained as women taking into account, consciously or not, their more limited reproductive opportunities (fifteen children at most) and the dependence of their offspring on male protection. Faithful men and unfaithful women, as well as promiscuity without intention to reproduce (a quite frequent phenomenon among humans, one should say) or, to the contrary, a celibate way of life, appear as perversions and require complicated ad hoc explanations as 'irrational' deviations from an otherwise biologically anchored 'human nature', unless an 'adaptive story' can be devised showing it to be functional for reproductive success after all.*

---

* A special case of biological reductionism is the decomposition of societies as 'cultures' into discrete nonorganic elements, called memes, following Richard Dawkins. Memes are imagined to be struggling with one another for existence and

Agentic Evolutionism

Looking back, I find in my own work on institutional change an example of a productive application of an evolutionary logic resembling that in *Origin*.* In an attempt to conceptualize gradual change as the normal condition of institutions – rather than as an exception interrupting 'normal' institutional stasis – my co-author and I hit on what we later called *imperfect reproduction*, which is easily recognized as just another name for Darwin's *descent with modification*. No biological reductionism was involved; the world we dealt with was and remained one of social action and social norms, not instincts and food shortage. The location where continuous institutional change originated was the gap between general rules and their application to specific situations. That application, we reasoned, must always be a creative act, as no rule can foresee all individual cases to which it is supposed to apply. Norms, in other words, must always be *interpreted* in relation to the conditions of the action they are supposed to govern before they can be enacted. Enactment can be either faithful or in bad faith, but either way it is not entirely preordained by the norm.

---

survival in host societies, like Dawkins' *selfish genes* are struggling for control over hoist organisms (Dawkins, *The Selfish Gene*, Oxford: Oxford University Press, 1989). Note the attribution of intentionality – 'egoism' – to both genes and memes, which are thought to use organisms and societies, respectively, as carriers securing their replication. This allows for truly exotic theorems. For example, why do religions, conceived as 'memeplexes', often include the 'prohibition of aberrant sexual practices such as incest, adultery, homosexuality, bestiality, castration, and religious prostitution'? Because this increases the chance of 'vertical transmission of the parent memeplex' (John D. Gottsch, 'Mutation, Selection, and Vertical Transmission of Theistic Memes in Religious Canons', *Journal of Memetics*, vol. 5, no. 1, 2001).

*   Wolfgang Streeck and Kathleen Thelen, 'Introduction: Institutional Change in Advanced Political Economies', in Streeck and Thelen, eds, *Beyond Continuity: Institutional Change in Advanced Political Economies*, Oxford: Oxford University Press, 2005, pp. 1–39.

Social structures, we pointed out, consist of norm-givers and norm-takers (who in a limiting case may be identical). Social norms are enforced by positive or negative sanctions dispensed by rulers, who may either be peers or specialized agents, like police, courts, or mafia thugs, commanding legal authority or superior means of violence, or both. (Rulers and ruled, connected as norm-givers and norm-takers, and as enforcers and appliers, together constitute what Max Weber calls a *Herrschaftsverband*, which may best be translated as 'regime'.) As norms are creatively applied, their interpretation – what they in practice 'mean' – is likely to drift. With time, norms are gradually refashioned through an evolving tradition, collective learning and precedents with respect to the sanctions that 'select' among legitimate and illegitimate interpretations, being modified in the everyday reproduction of social structure through social action. What practical applications norm-following gives rise to is unpredictable from the perspective of the norm; in this sense norm-following does operate as a stochastic source generating *variations* of and around a normatively coded practice, while sanctioning may appear as social *selection* of actions, comparable to natural selection of physical properties or instinctive behaviour in biological as distinguished from social evolutionism.

Note that there is no biology here and, just as in Darwin, no genetics – only actors and actions with different power and perspectives. There is, however, variation and selection, variation originating in the open-ended need to bridge the inevitable gap between the general and the specific, selection consisting in the application of institutionalized sanctions, the two connected in a relationship of social control. Change is endogenous and continuous, and revised institutions grow out of inherited ones, with society drawing on and limited to institutional material inherited from the past. Institutional change, in other words, is 'path-dependent'. That it is not a natural environment that does the selection but a structure of (formal or informal, legitimate or illegitimate) power or authority points to an important difference between a human society and a biological species. Societies, unlike species, are organized, typically in classes, and such organization intervenes between human individuals and humanity as a whole. Individual responses to the need for interactive interpretation and enactment of institutionalized social order are selected, not by Nature improving the species to help it survive, but by ruling classes identifying the interests of society with their own interests. Class interests, however, unlike biological survival interests, can be contested, and to the extent that they relate to modes of material production, they affect also the relationship between the human species and nature, and indeed the chances of survival of the former in the latter.

Does Society Make Leaps?

An exciting question inspired by *Origin* is whether human history is really as continuous, and social development as incremental, as natural history is under the Darwinian paradigm. Is it true that in human life as well there is just evolution, and no revolution? Is the progress of humanity really dependent on random mutations in the actualization of inherited patterns of social order, on the imperfect reproduction of institutions, and on collective selection, however accomplished, from its results, within the confines of the historical material, what biologists call 'phyletic constraints'?* Can there not in human history be 'pathbreaking' new ideas conceived in creative moral or technical reasoning, ideas enabling humanity to perform the very revolutionary leaps that nature, according to Darwin, can never and will never make? I cannot even try to answer these questions here. But I note that, interestingly, they are being asked also among evolutionary biologists, who try to make

---

* Stephen Jay Gould and R. C. Lewontin. 'The Spandrels of San Marco and the Panglossian Paradigm: A Critique of the Adaptationist Programme', *Proc. R. Soc. Lond. B.*, vol. 205, no. 1161, 1979, pp. 581–98.

sense of the fact that there may have been periods in natural history when evolutionary gradualism was 'punctuated', in that it rapidly accelerated until it again slowed down.*

I also suggest that whether or not the evolution of life proceeds in fits and starts – and whether the possibility of revolution in social affairs ends the analogy between human and natural history – there is good reason not to underestimate the extent of continuity or overestimate the potential of disruption in social life, and to be careful not to give too much weight in social theory (and in social practice as well) to idealistic voluntarism. As none less than Alexis de Tocqueville argued in his book *The Old Regime and the French Revolution*,† what during and immediately after a revolutionary moment may appear as an entirely new society, one without historical precedent, may with some distance be recognized as an outcome of long-running trends of gradual social transformation. Moreover, revolutionaries who have come to power are more often than not shocked to learn that while they may have taken possession of some of their society's institutions – in modern times, in particular, of the state – other institutions have successfully resisted their attempts at conquering. Also, action on the ground, the repertoire of creative compliance with inevitably underdetermined institutions – the supply of imperfect norm enactments from which institutions must select – does not necessarily change in tune with new political power relations. As

---

* Niles Eldredge and Stephen Jay Gould, 'Punctuated Equilibria: An Alternative to Phyletic Gradualism', in T. J. M. Schopf, ed., *Models In Paleobiology*, San Francisco: Freeman Cooper, 1972. This debate has entered into social science theories of institutional change precisely where a way was sought to get out of the conservatism of path dependence and allow for creative interruptions in moments of spontaneous creation, with the equilibrium of incremental adjustment being 'punctuated' in 'formative moments' at 'critical junctures'. For an instructive application to a substantive problem of institutional analysis, see Stephen D. Krasner, 'Sovereignty: An Institutional Perspective', *Comparative Political Studies*, vol. 21, 1988, pp. 66–94.

† Alexis de Tocqueville, *The Old Regime and the French Revolution*, New York: Anchor, 1983 [1856].

that supply cannot be completely controlled from above, not even with terrorist means, even revolutionary change is always embedded in tradition and historical continuity.*

Similar reasoning may be applied to the role of ideas in society and history, from cognitive images to normative precepts. Darwinian evolutionism suggests a conceptual framework in which societies store, replenish, update and generate a wide range of different ideas that those in a position to do so can select. Is the production of ideas a process of stochastic mutation? Scientists and philosophers, who in modern societies occupy the high-culture tier of ideational discourse, will insist that their thinking at least is far from 'wild' and is to the contrary strictly disciplined by logic and observation. From the perspective of a society's 'ruling ideas', however, the current production of new, competing ideas can only appear chaotic. To established 'old thinking', any 'new thinking' must seem eccentric, 'radical', and even ridiculous, and its evolution anarchic in the sense of both unpredictable and ungovernable.† While new ideas necessarily descend from a tradition and would in fact be literally inconceivable outside of it, here too descent always comes with modification, since the way tradition is interpreted and appropriated is never predetermined. Moreover, as ideas change faster than structures, and are less costly to produce

---

* Which is best recognized with hindsight. See the despair of the victorious Bolsheviks in the 1920s on the resilience of Russia's agrarian hinterland, followed almost a century later by complaints after the end of communism about the 'mentality' of the Russian people still being shaped by their Stalinist past (Svetlana Alexievich, *Secondhand Time: The Last of the Soviets*, New York: Random House, 2016). See also the discussion in and outside Germany after 1945 on whether the West German Federal Republic was in fact a new state and society or just the same old Germany differently dressed. While there was change, there was certainly also a lot of continuity, which became a political cause in the 1950s and 1960s for the emerging intellectual Left.

† Thomas S. Kuhn, *The Structure of Scientific Revolutions*, Chicago: University of Chicago Press, 1962.

than new institutions or new factories, society's ideational endowment not only exceeds current institutional needs but will inevitably be internally diverse and contradictory. This is so in spite of continuous attempts by ruling classes to limit the provision of new ideas to ones that they consider as following logically and legitimately from the old, established ideas enforced and controlled by them. To this extent at least, the Darwinian model of endogenous random mutation and exogenous environmental selection seems quite applicable also to the world of evolving ideas and ideologies.

Speciation and Specialization: Smith, Darwin, Durkheim (and Marx as Well)

Another intriguing question that comes up when reading *Origin* is what corresponds among humans and human societies to biological speciation as conceived by Darwin. Darwin suggests that of the variations among an organism's offspring, those that stand the best chance of survival – in the sense of successful reproduction – are most different from their parents and siblings, and therefore most likely to develop into new species. This is because speciation in Darwin is essentially niche-seeking: the more organisms differ, the less likely they are to depend on the same resource base. Variation, then, is a way of escaping from competition and thereby easing the 'struggle for existence'; it is in this sense a 'strategy' to prevail in that struggle by avoiding it.

Sociologists are aware, or should be, that this figure of thought strongly influenced none less than Émile Durkheim in his attempt to understand what he,* following Adam Smith,† called the

---

* Émile Durkheim, *The Division of Labour in Society*, New York: The Free Press, 1964 [1893].

† Adam Smith, *An Inquiry into the Nature and Causes of the Wealth of Nations*, Oxford: Oxford University Press, 1993 [1776].

'division of labour' – in more modern language, the structural differentiation of complex societies. Rejecting economistic-hedonistic explanations, Durkheim suggested that rather than the pursuit of happiness, it was the fear of a Hobbesian war of all against all that made people specialize, in search of ways to make a living that did not pitch them into head-to-head competition with others and thereby tear society apart.* Drawing explicitly on Darwin, Durkheim dissociates himself from the utilitarianism of economic theory by explaining the division of labour in society as a response to rising 'dynamic density' in a social space, caused by either growing population or shrinking territory, with specialization serving to maintain social peace and for this reason becoming a moral obligation.†

Comparing Durkheim to Darwin also reveals, in addition to the commonality of niche-seeking in search of protection from competitive pressure, important differences between social and natural life. What is *speciation* in nature is *specialization* in society – the former producing new species, the latter taking place within one and the same species, substituting for speciation and thereby allowing humanity to remain united. A corollary is that differentiation in society can progress incomparably faster than in nature, where it requires change, drawn out over generations, in biological substructures. Another is that variation within the human species – social rather than biological variation – can produce more, and more easily adaptable, diversity than variation within other species. This was noted already by Adam Smith in his comparison, in *Wealth of Nations*, between two dogs of different breeds and two humans in different occupations:

Many tribes of animals acknowledged to be all of the same species, derive from nature a much more remarkable distinction

---

* Durkheim, *Division of Labour*, Book II, chapters I and II.
† Durkheim, *Division of Labour*, pp. 208–09.

of genius, than what, antecedent to custom and education, appears to take place among men. By nature a philosopher is not in genius and disposition half so different from a street porter, as a mastiff is from a greyhound, or a greyhound from a spaniel, or this last from a shepherd's dog.*

Although philosophers and street porters are more *physically* alike than mastiffs and greyhounds – which are so different, due to human rather than natural selection, that they, following Darwin, might under conditions of spatial separation evolve into different species – *functionally* they are equally different or even more so. Remarkably for his time, Smith concludes from this that social differentiation must be the result not of different physical capacities but of socialization, in particular of different opportunities for individuals from families with different positions in the social structure.†

Biological speciation and social specialization differ in yet another way, also commented upon by Smith. Dogs, Smith observes, cannot use their different biological capacities for mutual benefit, because they are unable to engage in exchange and cooperation. In fact, dogs, and animals generally, are essentially lonely: they must be capable of doing by themselves everything they need to do to survive and procreate‡ – an idea found also in the

---

* Smith, *Wealth of Nations*, p. 24.

† 'The difference of natural talents in different men is, in reality, much less than we are aware of . . . The difference between the most dissimilar characters, between a philosopher and a common street porter, for example, seems to arise not so much from nature as from habit, custom, and education. When they came into the world, and for the first six or eight years of their existence, they were, perhaps, very much alike, and neither their parents nor playfellows could perceive any remarkable difference. About that age, or soon after, they come to be employed in very different occupations. The difference of talents comes then to be taken notice of, and widens by degrees, till at last the vanity of the philosopher is willing to acknowledge scarce any resemblance'. Smith, *Wealth of Nations*, pp. 23–24.

‡ 'The effects of those different geniuses and talents, for want of the power and disposition to barter and exchange, cannot be brought into a common stock . . . Each

anthropological reflections of the young Karl Marx. Humans, by comparison, acting on meaning rather than behaving by instinct, can set up far-flung networks of cooperative relations with other humans – social structures and normative orders that allow and encourage them to make themselves dependent on the cooperation of others by specializing far beyond what the need of animal organisms for individual autarky would permit. It is this capacity for other-reliant and other-dependent social identity formation by which the human actor becomes, so Marx following Aristotle, a *zoon politicón* – a political animal, and indeed the only animal that is political.*

Of course, sociologists know about the profound fragility and vulnerability of social structures built on but not anchored in the generalist biological substructure of humanity; they are aware of the possibility of such structures becoming anomic, that is, destructive of the trust they require, or asymmetrical and exploitative of the human ability, and indeed need, for cooperation and social integration; and they concern themselves with how institutions in crisis may be repaired or replaced in and through politics – by ensuring cooperation against exploitation – if catastrophic breakdowns of social order are to be avoided. It was not just Marx but also Durkheim who insisted that the institutionalization of the division of labour within the single human species, uniquely promising of human and material progress, may be fatally deficient if it is lacking, above all, in 'justice'.†

---

animal is still obliged to support and defend itself, separately and independently, and derives no sort of advantage from that variety of talents with which nature has distinguished its fellows'. Smith, *Wealth of Nations*, p. 24.

* Karl Marx, *Grundrisse der Kritik der Politischen Ökonomie (Rohentwurf) 1857–1858*, Berlin: Dietz Verlag, 1953 [1857–58], p. 6: 'The human being is in the most literal sense a ζῷον πολιτικόν, not merely a gregarious animal, but an animal which can individuate itself only in the midst of society'.

† Durkheim, *Division of Labour*, p. 322.

Darwin's analysis of biological speciation in *Origin* teaches us by extension about the peculiarities of the human being, biologically a generalist who, through socialization and social organization, bests all biological specialists – the invincible super-decathlete of the natural universe. Humans, uniquely among complex organisms, are capable of surviving in the Arctic as well as the Kalahari, on the Amazon and in New York City, travelling faster, diving longer distances, and flying higher than any other animal, and all of this without having to split up into different, differently specialized species.* Society and its institutions enable humans to live as 'moral animals',† free from the dictates of instincts and the constraints of physical inheritance, both forced and empowered to make choices, and relieved of the need, when confronting new challenges, to hope for the creeping progress of

---

* This was already known two and a half thousand years ago. See for example Sophocles, *Antigone*:

> Numberless are the world's wonders, but none
> More wonderful than man; the stormgray sea
> Yields to his prows, the huge crests bear him high . . .
> The lightboned birds and beasts that cling to cover,
> The lithe fish lighting their reaches of dim water,
> All are taken, tamed in the net of his mind;
> The lion on the hill, the wild horse windy-maned,
> Resign to him; and his blunt yoke has broken
> The sultry shoulders of the mountain bull.
> Words also, and thought as rapid as air,
> He fashions to his good use; statecraft is his . . .
> O clear intelligence, force beyond all measure!
> O fate of man, working both good and evil!
> When the laws are kept, how proudly his city stands!

Sophocles, *Antigone*, in *The Oedipus Cycle: An English Version*, trans. Dudley Fitts and Robert Fitzgerald, New York: Harcourt, Brace, 1939.

† Charles Darwin, *The Descent of Man, and Selection in Relation to Sex*, London: John Murray, 1871. See also Geoffrey M. Hodgson, *From Pleasure Machines to Moral Communities: An Evolutionary Economics without Homo Economicus*, Chicago: University of Chicago Press, 2013.

biological mutation and selection. Of course, here we are faced
with another daunting question – namely, how what surely seems
a categorical difference between humans and other animals could
possibly have come about through gradual and continuous change,
without nature taking leaps, as it cannot under Darwin's iron law
of historical continuity. All we can do here is speculate about a
very long and, at first, very slow, although later perhaps accelerating, evolutionary process in which the grip of biologically rooted
instincts on the human species became progressively relaxed, freeing up general capacities available for specialization and making
space for society to gradually take control of increasingly biologically deregulated beings, to guide them out of natural history and
into human history.*

The 'Struggle for Existence' and the Immortality of Society

The difference between speciation and specialization as responses
to competition in the 'struggle for existence' reflects also on the
notion of 'survival of the fittest'. For Darwin, survival meant
survival into the next, always slightly modified generation – or in
other words, successful reproduction. Natural selection in *Origin*
was concerned with individuals, not with groups: what does or
does not 'survive' is not the species but its various members, some
of them on the way to evolving into species of their own. In human
life, there is also selection of individuals, but socially rather than
biologically, with society and its institutions selecting, by positive
or negative sanctions, among different performances of institutionalized expectations. Biological capacities do play a role,
although not the only, and not even a dominant one: he or she

---

* One implication of gradualism here is that there cannot have been a first society.
Each society has a predecessor and thus a tradition, the latter consisting in the earliest
societies of the instincts of their biological past, in the process of receding and making
space for their replacement with social norms and institutions.

who lacks the physical equipment needed to run the 10,000 metres at the Olympics can always try to be selected as a moral philosopher or, if this doesn't work either, a street porter (or, today, a truck driver).

Social Darwinism, by comparison, is concerned also with group selection, that is, with 'peoples' that come, inevitably, organized as societies. In this nineteenth-century worldview, it is above all these among which there is 'struggle for existence'.* Most likely to prevail in that struggle, according to the Social Darwinist tradition, are societies that allow for and actively enforce rigorous Darwinian selection among their members, reproducing at their microlevel of social interaction the law of the stronger that they collectively face at the macro-level of international relations – letting the weak fall by the wayside for the strong to survive, thereby enabling the society as a whole to do the same.†

Among the many things that social scientists may have to say on this is that societies rarely die – apart from very small ones that can be physically extinguished by genocide or natural disaster. Normally enough members survive, even in extreme circumstances, to make what may at first look like the end of a society appear from a distance as a step – however transformative – in a more or less continuous historical process.‡ Beyond a certain size and complexity, societies, instead of dying, reform, reorganize,

---

* The modern term for this in international relations theory is 'realism'. It can to some extent point to Max Weber as theoretical inspiration. Weber saw the international sphere of his time as an arena of unmitigated conflict among nation-states whose collective ambitions far exceeded what was available for sharing between them, for example 'virgin lands' waiting to be colonized. Parliamentary party democracy for Weber was primarily a training ground for educating future national leaders in the struggle for power.

† Herbert Spencer, *The Principles of Sociology in Three Volumes*, ed. Jonathan H. Turner, ed., New Brunswick and London: Transaction Publishers, 2003 [1883], vol. II, chapters XVII, XVIII).

‡ Patricia A. McAnany and Norman Yoffee, eds, *Questioning Collapse: Human Resilience, Ecological Vulnerability, and the Aftermath of Empire*, New York: Cambridge University Press, 2010.

restructure – and not just as a result of defeat at the hands of other societies or because of resource shortages. Indeed, what are death and survival for a society – what collapse and what structural adjustment – even its members may define differently, depending on their position in the social structure. Human societies have no single, unified, fixed purpose, though Social Darwinists, in alliance incidentally with standard economics, may try to convince us of the opposite. While death and survival are unambiguously defined for biological organisms, including human individuals, their definition is messy at best for human societies, which are organized around social meanings and social norms and can therefore be both differently defined as well as rapidly restructured. For example, what marked the end of the Roman Empire for the senatorial class in Rome was nothing short of its glorious rebirth for a Germanic prince like Theodoric the Great, who in the sixth century CE assumed the Roman emperorship in addition to his Gothic kingship.

Complexity as Destiny?

Finally, reading *Origins* may prompt us to reflect on the notion of progress and what it could mean in both nature and society. As pointed out, evolutionary improvement for Darwin is fundamentally only relative: evolution means adjustment, *within the limits of the possible,* to an essentially unpredictably changing natural environment, inanimate and animate. What adjustment is possible is limited by the insuperable condition of gradualism and the phyletic constraints imposed by past natural history. This renders evolution a sequence of instant improvisations that serve their adaptive 'function' as best they can while likely to be suboptimal in comparison to what, if possible, could be newly designed 'from scratch' for the purpose at hand. In some cases, such improvisations might appear to be regressive; an example being whales that have no need any more for the legs of their landed ancestors, which are as a consequence reduced to useless bones loosely attached to their pelvis and visible only to the anatomist. Consider also the human body and its many suboptimal features for a bipedal animal, resulting among other things in frequent back pain and headaches and an inordinate share of brainpower having to be devoted just to walking. It seems reasonable to see here a parallel to the path-dependency of human history and the constraints it imposes on institutional change.

But does this mean that there is no directionality at all in evolution, no general trend? Sometimes the Darwin of *Origin*, perhaps in an occasional slip of the pen, seems to be talking about something like *absolute* perfection, without being very explicit.* What does come to mind here, at least for the modern reader, is the notion of complexity. Is the history of life not a history of the evolution of increasingly complex organisms, meaning internally differentiated as well as connected, from the single-cell amoeba to the human being with its unimaginably complex brain? And is the same not true for the history of human society and its evolution from roaming family bands to the networked global humanity of today? Is there, in other words, an inherent tendency, or even pressure, in both biological and social structures to grow ever more complex?

However we may tend to answer such questions, we may want to keep two insights in mind. One, the biggest share of the world's biomass (still?) consists of single-cell organisms† that seem to be

---

* 'Recent forms are generally looked at as being, in some vague sense, higher than ancient and extinct forms; and they are in so far higher as the later and more improved forms have conquered the older and less improved organic beings in the struggle for life' (*Origin*, p. 512). And less vague: 'As natural selection works solely by and for the good of each being, all corporal and mental endowments will tend to progress towards perfection' (p. 526).

† 'The combined domains of archaea and bacteria make up the most diverse and abundant group of organisms on Earth and inhabit practically all environments where the temperature is below +140°C. They are found in water, soil, air, as the microbiome of an organism, hot springs and even deep beneath the Earth's crust in rocks. The

quite comfortable with themselves, apparently lacking any desire to join together in pursuit of higher complexity. Perhaps a parallel at the human level could be 'primitive' societies and subsistence economies that might have gone on as such for thousands more years had not the more 'complex' societies of Europe made a continuation of their independent, distinct way of life impossible. In both cases, what a theory of complexity as the ultimate *telos* of natural and human history would have to explain is what the German philosopher Ernst Bloch called, in a different context, *die Gleichzeitigkeit des Ungleichzeitigen* (the coexistence of past and present, within the present). And two, we may want to consider the possibility, at least at the level of human society, of the historical drive for complexity, to the extent that there is one, going too far and, as perhaps under global capitalism, becoming dangerous to humanity's health. In this case, 'regression' to the reduced complexity of parallel, 'segmental' societies – smaller and independently self-governed, related, in Durkheim's terms, through mechanic rather than organic solidarity, thus keeping themselves simple although, hopefully, not too simple – may be the real progress of humankind at this stage of human history. At least there is nothing in *Origin* to rule this out.

---

number of prokaryotes is estimated to be around five million trillion trillion, or 5×10^{30}, accounting for at least half the biomass on Earth', from the entry 'Microorganism' on Wikipedia, 26 February 2018. For more detail see William B. Whitman, David C. Coleman and William J. Wiebe, 'Prokaryotes: The Unseen Majority', *Proceedings of the National Academy of Sciences*, vol. 95, no. 12, 1998, pp. 6578–83.

Appendix: Letters from Europe

L ETTER FROM EUROPE is the title of a monthly column written since May 2017 for the online Spanish journal *El Salto*. The whole series is available in Spanish and English (translated by Carlos Prieto del Campo) on my blog, wolfgang-streeck.com/carta-desde-europa. The following are the six letters published between December 2019 and May 2020.

15 December 2019
Getting serious

In the last week of November the European Parliament declared a 'climate emergency' for the European Union – a classic case of symbolic politics with no consequences, conceived solely for the benefit of Fridays for Future. Meanwhile, behind the facade, momentous decisions were being fought over that had nothing to do with climate change, except that they will require not billions but trillions of euros. This is money that will be sorely missed in the battle against global warming and the social effects of neoliberal austerity.

What is at issue is European armament. A nasty fight is going on among France, Germany and the United States over an old question: the relationship between 'Europe' and NATO. Should European countries contribute their military forces to NATO, where they would effectively be under American command? Or should they integrate their forces into some European 'defence' entity that would then be either a consolidated 'European pillar' of NATO or a 'European army', perhaps allied with the US or perhaps not, but in any case under 'European' command, whatever this might be?

The story, here much simplified, begins with the unanimous commitment of NATO members in 2002, confirmed in 2014, to raise their military expenditures to two per cent of their GDP. Essentially the addressee was Germany, whose defence budget was and still is no more than roughly half of this. France and the UK, both nuclear powers, have long met the target due to the high cost of nuclear bombs, bombers, submarines and aircraft carriers. Conventional troops are cheap by comparison, but if you have to pay for nukes there may still not be enough money left for them. When the 2002 resolution was passed, the United States was busy making Putin's Russia the successor of the Soviet Union as the archenemy of 'the West'. The obvious intention was to bring back the good old days of Yeltsin from 1990 to 1999 when Russia, with its huge reserves of natural resources, was a favourite hunting ground for American business, very much like Ukraine is today.

In military terms, Russia is no more than a minor player, leaving aside its nuclear weaponry. If Germany did spend two per cent of its GDP on its military, its 'defence' budget – Germany's alone! – would be about 40 per cent higher than that of Russia. As an alliance, even without the United States, NATO is so superior to Russia that a Russian attack on Western Europe is simply inconceivable; it would amount to willful suicide. This might be why the 2002 pledge was not taken seriously by European countries, including Germany.

Enter Trump. It seems that originally Trump tried an isolationist foreign policy, extricating the United States from foreign entanglements to please his Midwestern voters. But this was sabotaged by the 'deep state' of the US military complex in alliance with American oil and gas interests. Today, while the United States still doesn't care much about NATO, it does care about Eastern Europe, as a pressure point against Russia and for geostrategic reasons related to the Western end of China's New Silk Road. If Europe refuses to take part or is (rightly) afraid of being hit if the US's Russia strategy were to go wrong, the American government is willing to act on its own, relying on its huge military presence in Germany and on troops currently stationed in the Baltics and in Poland.

Today both Germany and France have lost confidence in the United States as a European ally. But France has a nuclear capacity (four submarines, one aircraft carrier, a bomber fleet) whereas Germany, squeezed between the four nuclear powers of the US, the UK, France and Russia, does not. France has little interest in Eastern Europe while Germany needs it as a market and an extended workbench for its manufacturing industry. What Eastern Europe is for Germany, Western Africa is for France; there, it is involved in several postcolonial wars that it is losing. The United States cannot be asked for help as it has its own interests in the region; so France needs 'Europe', meaning a more heavily armed Germany supplying ground troops for 'anti-terrorist' warfare, conducted under French diplomatic protection on the UN Security Council where, post-Brexit, France is the only EU member with a permanent seat and a veto.

This puts Germany in an uncomfortable position. Macron, seeking 'strategic autonomy', rhetorically for 'Europe' but *de facto* for France, wants Germany to contribute its two per cent to an EU army instead of to NATO. And so, getting impatient over German procrastination, Macron declares NATO 'brain-dead'. He seeks accommodation with Putin, publicly wondering why Russia should be considered an enemy in the first place, and blocking the extension of the EU to the West Balkans. But France also continues to let it be known that the French nuclear umbrella cannot be extended to other countries, not even to Germany. If push were to come to shove, Paris would not be sacrificed for Berlin. The United States, on the other hand, has promised to defend Germany with nuclear arms if neces-sary; it was on this quid pro quo that Germany signed the nuclear nonproliferation treaty of 1968. Doubts about the agreement have always persisted, and attempts to assuage them were a running story through postwar German foreign policy. Now, with Trump, such doubts are stronger than ever.

Hope still exists among the German political elites that after Trump things will return to what was deemed normal in the past. But most consider this unlikely. Still, hardly anyone in the German foreign policy establishment, apart perhaps from diehard Franco-German 'special relationship' European inte-grationists, wants the country to be second-in-command in a French-dominated ersatz NATO. Presently a majority seem to be willing to live with the risks of American anti-Putinism, including the risk of Russia modernizing its nuclear arsenal to balance a German conventional build-up. On the other hand, Germany cannot afford a split with France, if only because the appearance of a German-French *entente cordial* helps hide Germany's hegemonic position in the EU. So, yes on a European army, but only as a 'European pillar' of NATO, and not as a step towards an independent, French-led third force equidistant between the United States and China.

There is space for lots of ambiguity here that can be used to hide the deep rift with France. But while Merkel was always a grandmaster in duplicity, her successors, whoever they may be, won't be able to match her. (If there was a political constant in Merkel, it was her loyalty to the United States; remember that as opposition leader she demanded that Germany join the American invasion of Iraq.) What is already clear is that Germany's refusal, in fact, inability, to choose in favour of France and 'Europe' and against the US and NATO makes it impossible for Germany to help Macron compensate for his domestic weakness by allowing him to present himself to the French public as the secret ruler of Europe and, by implication, Germany. Keeping Macron in power for another term has, from the moment he was elected, been one of the central objectives of German European policy.

The future of 'European integration' is becoming murkier by the day.

15 January 2020
Post-Brexit, post-Labour?

In a few days, Brexit will be history and the negotiations about a trade agreement between the newly sovereign United Kingdom and what is left of the EU will begin. It is quite possible that the EU will again choose to play hardball and drag out the process, leading to another game of 'no deal' chicken. It is also quite possible that the supranational centralists still have not understood the lessons of the Brexit struggle and its outcome.

Even more important may be the utter devastation suffered by the Labour Party in the December election. Labour is now about to join other social-democratic parties in Europe on their march into irrelevance. The Corbyn project, so crucial for the European Left, is dead, and very likely forever. The attempt to rejuvenate socialism by binding together the traditional working class and the social movements of the victims of neoliberal 'reform' has dismally failed. Did it have to? In hindsight, it collapsed before it could really be tested, due to a massive strategic blunder of the Corbyn leadership: underestimating the significance of national sovereignty for left politics under globalization and trying to be on both sides at the same time in the battle over Brexit.

Not that Corbyn's job had been an easy one, and perhaps there was no good solution for him. While Labour's core constituencies had voted 'Leave' in the referendum, the Blairites and the 'cosmopolitan' section of the middle-class, fascinated with 'Europe' as a symbol of social modernity and political purity, passionately supported 'Remain'. From the referendum to the electoral disaster of 2019, the Labour leadership tried to downplay the issue of sovereignty and skirted the question of what side it was on, hoping that this would keep the party united and make Labour electable for Leavers and Remainers alike. This was neither fish nor fowl. In the end the Remainers suspected that a Labour government might leave whereas the Leavers feared it might remain. So the party lost on both sides of a political divide that had so dramatically disunited the United Kingdom.

One can now see how catastrophically the Labour Party, even under Corbyn, misread the mood of the left-behind old or not-so-old working class. Two points stand out in particular. One is that the party never understood the depth of the determination among these voters to no longer allow their national government to enlist 'Brussels' or international summit meetings or European courts or 'the world market' as an excuse for refusing to protect their interests. Voters, especially those dependent on an active interventionist state, wanted to be reassured that the state of the United Kingdom was their state, not the state of international markets or globalizing technocrats. To this extent, Brexit was about nothing less than the restoration of political accountability and trust in political leadership after the excuses of the Third Way. In downplaying its significance Labour risked and lost the little trust that had remained, as well as what Corbyn had rebuilt during his short tenure.

Second, Labour had somehow failed to comprehend the extent of the cultural cleavage between the old working and the new middle class. Until Election Day, Labour strategists expected voters in the working class constituencies of Northern England to vote Labour despite the party's wavering on Brexit, simply because they could never bring themselves to vote for the Tories. This underestimated the strength of working class conservatism and patriotism. It also overlooked the emotional wreckage caused by the attacks of a new left denouncing those who wanted Brexit to help them protect their accustomed way of life as xenophobic, homophobic, misogynic, racist, 'Little Englanders'. A party whose cultural elites consider its traditional supporters down-in-their-hearts fascists cannot hope to retain their confidence. As in so many other countries, replacing class in political discourse with identity caused an identitarian backlash from those for whom the national state has remained a principal focus of collective identification.

The election of 12 December may have sealed the divorce between the British working class and its traditional party; it may also have realigned British politics. If Boris Johnson is the cunning political animal that he sometimes seems to be, he may try to turn the pro-Brexit working class voters into pro-British Tory voters, and he may succeed. This would require him to move from the neoliberalism of his years of political apprenticeship to a one-nation Toryism in the Disraeli tradition, as was tried in vain by his hapless predecessor, Theresa May. If he could win his party for this – and he will for a long time be the only prime minister they have got – it would pull the floor from under Labour's feet. To secure Tory rule for the next two or more decades, Johnson may even let the Scots go their way, thereby creating a natural Tory majority in what would remain of the United Kingdom. Labour could then join the Liberal Democrats to celebrate together with them a 'woke' cosmopolitan lifestyle, competing for the representation of all kinds of minorities and for the votes of what the French call the bobos: the bourgeois bohemians of the big cities.

15 February 2020
Now Germany

> Things fall apart; the centre cannot hold;
> Mere anarchy is loosed upon the world
> *W. B. Yeats*

Angela Merkel's *Götterdämmerung* is dragging on, and it is not a happy affair. When her heir apparent, AKK, found it impossible to do the impossible – enforce on her party, down to the smallest village, a watertight boycott on the elected representatives of ten to fifteen per cent of the voters – she was finished in cold blood by her one-time patron, with a long-distance shot fired from a press conference in South Africa. Now Merkel's succession is again wide open, and her chances of holding on to the chancellorship until the end of her term one-and-a-half years from now have never been better.

As of mid-February, the situation on the German political battlefield is changing by the day, and this may continue for some time. The only constant is the German constitution and the enormous power it affords the chancellor. A sitting chancellor can be removed only by a so-called 'constructive vote of non-confidence', meaning that the Bundestag must elect a successor with more than half of its members. This is unthinkable, if only because the SPD, while known for deep political ineptitude, won't help the CDU contest the 2021 elections with an incumbent chancellor. Nor can there be early elections as this requires the chancellor to ask for and lose a vote of non-confidence; Merkel, like Schröder, could arrange for this, but she won't. So, the question becomes: who wants to succeed AKK as party chair and chancellor-candidate and become the next sitting duck for the next potshot fired from the chancellery if he or she fails to meet Merkel's demanding expectations? Expect a year at least of anarchic power battles, some open, most covert, with lots of casualties. 2020 may see the falling apart of the last centrist governing party in Europe.

For Europe, this means more indecision, for a much longer time than had been anticipated. Nobody knows how the Merkel experiment – de facto turning party into presidential government – will work out. With succession struggles raging in the CDU and CSU and between them, it is unclear what Merkel could promise her European partners that she might still be able to wring support for, from a parliamentary party not knowing who will control their reselection in 2021.

Issues on hand include the negotiations with Britain over its future relationship with the EU (will Germany be able to defend the interests of its export industries and prevent Brussels, in particular France, from taking too hard a line on the United Kingdom?), the budget of the EU after Brexit (to what extent will Germany have to fill the gaps caused by the British departure?), the separate budget for the Eurozone, as insisted upon by Macron, the military cooperation with France and the relationship between the EU and NATO (who will prevail in Germany, the 'Gaullists' or the Atlanticists'?), etc.

Why was AKK's mission an impossible one? The CDU under Merkel had turned into a party of technocratic-neoliberal modernization: a third way party of the centre-right. Like the SPD earlier, it became increasingly unable to manage the tensions between the winners and losers of economic and cultural restructuring for international 'competitiveness'. On the centre-left the losers went from the SPD to the Linkspartei, at least for a while; on the centre-right they moved to the AfD. In the German political system with its multiple levels of proportionate political representation, from village to Federal Republic, the AfD, with time also attracting former SPD voters, soon became an established party, winning between 10 and 15 per cent of the vote nation-wide.

It has long been a strategic mantra of the CDU that there should be no political space on its right for another party; after the open border episode in 2015 this finally became unrealistic. The representation gap caused by the CDU abandoning its conservative constituency was increasingly filled by the AfD, a mixed bag of grumpy conservatives and right-wing extremists, struggling for control over their party while seeking to attract CDU, SPD and non-voters. In response, after some to and fro, the CDU declared the AfD untouchable – a strategy in which all other parties joined. The assumption was that a party excluded as fascist from the constitutional spectrum would be for all political purposes non-existent. Simultaneously Merkel was reinforcing her effort to compensate for her party's dwindling support on the right by forging a coalition with the Greens, given that the SPD had begun to melt away due to decades of third way junior partnership with the CDU. While the prospect of CDU government forever was to assuage the CDU's remaining traditionalists, the neutralization through Nazification of the AfD and its voters would keep the new party small enough to allow for the continuation of what Merkel calls 'market-conforming democracy'.

This did not work in Thuringia, a long-time CDU stronghold, and became increasingly unlikely to work elsewhere. In the Thuringian election of 2019 the CDU was down by 11.8 percentage points, winning only 21.7 per cent, less than the

AfD at 23.4 per cent. The other centrist parties ended up close to extinction: the SPD at 8.2 (-4.2), the Greens at 5.2 (-0.5), and the Liberals at 5.0 (+2.5). The winner was the Linkspartei at 31.0 per cent (+2.8), mostly due to a likable minister-president who would fit just as well in the SPD. The two outcast parties from the perspective of the CDU, AfD and Linkspartei together gained an absolute majority of 54.4 per cent. This excluded the CDU from any governing majority as long as it stuck to its boycott of the AfD and, of course, Die Linke; allowing the latter to govern in order to maintain distance from the former seems to have been suggested by Berlin but was unacceptable to local party members. In the event Merkel's insistence on isolating the AfD, not even permitting a centre-right minority government tolerated by it, caused a revolt in her party about which we know two things: it will not end soon, and its effects will be lasting.

Remarkably, the unending public debate on Thüringen never went beyond party-political tactics; nobody asks who had voted for the AfD or why. Research shows that AfD voters came from all parties, including the party of non-voters (turnout, at 65 per cent, was high for a regional election). Did all of them share all of the views of the many unsavory characters among the AfD leadership? 60 per cent of the voters in 2019 voted for their party of choice 'out of conviction' and 34 per cent out of 'disappointment' with other parties; the numbers include the AfD voters, of whom only 39 per cent said they voted out of conviction while 53 per cent voted out of disappointment.

Will stigmatizing them win AfD voters back for the centre or the left? By age group, the AfD was overrepresented among the young, especially among young males; of 18 to 24 year-old men, 30 per cent voted AfD, as did 32 per cent of those aged 25 to 34. The *Linkspartei*, almost symmetrically, was the party of the old: until age 44 its share was 24 per cent or less; only above age 60 (38 per cent and more) did it do disproportionately well.

What were the concerns which the CDU of Angela Merkel and the Linkspartei, not to mention the SPD on its deathbed, were unable to address, so that a historically revisionist party of the right could thrive on them? 83 per cent of AfD voters in Thuringia agreed to, and only 16 per cent disagreed with, the statement, 'I am very worried that our life in Germany is changing too much'. While this is high, remarkably 37 per cent of CDU voters, and even 30 per cent of Green voters, felt the same. Leaving it to the radical right to represent popular demands for 'taking back control', in the hope thereby to lock the losers of competitive modernization out of legitimate politics, may badly backfire.

15 March 2020
All bets off

Corona hit the EU unprepared – but what wouldn't? Only a few weeks ago, a little less than a year after the so-called 'European elections' of 2019, the Brussels crowd were still puzzling over what its outcome was to mean in real life, apart from four new 'presidents'. There was the usual haggling over the budget, now post-Brexit: 1.0 per cent of aggregate GDP as now, 1.049 per cent as proposed by the Commission, 1.074 per cent as suggested by the president of the Council, 1.114 per cent as demanded by the countries benefitting from the 'structural funds', or 1.300 per cent (!) as envisaged by the 'parliament'. (Average government spending among EU member states is 45.6 per cent.) Now that the global economy appears to be moving into the next recession, it seems impossible to estimate the denominator, let alone the numerator, of the future EU spending ratio.

Another issue, now also almost forgotten, was what the PR staff of the new Commission president, von der Leyen, has labelled a 'Green Deal': an exercise in dressing up old budget items, in particular under the Common Agricultural Policy (CAP), as new spending on the environment. There were also preparations under way for the next round of Brexit negotiations, planned to be concluded in the summer, with France and the 'parliament' pressing for maximally humiliating terms for the UK, including an obligation to accept the jurisdiction of the European Court of Justice in trade disputes – a barely disguised attempt to bring down the Johnson government with a renewed threat of a 'hard Brexit'. And, in addition, there were debates whether the EU should take in and distribute over its member countries 1,500 unaccompanied minors and sick children (it was said: preferably girls) from the Greek refugee camps, a remarkably minimalist act of charity designed, clearly, to make journalists and the public forget about the EU's failure to make any constructive contribution to peace in Syria, not to mention Libya, thrown into chaos by French and British military intervention.

Then came the virus, and EU politics went into something like a coma, the date of reawakening uncertain. As a last sign of life the Commission, pressed by France and Germany, insisted that countries keep their borders open, public health worries notwithstanding. As they sealed off cities like Milan and undertook to segregate small children from their grandparents, member states were ordered not to seal themselves off from one another, in order to maintain 'European solidarity'. Of course, nobody listens. Even Germany, Merkel's murky pseudo-internationalist rhetoric notwithstanding, has stepped up controls at its border with, of all countries, France – much to the dismay of Macron who believes in 'a sovereign France in a sovereign Europa', symbolized by free French movement across the Rhine. In the dream world of Macron and Brussels, whatever the cost, there can be no circuit breakers, firewalls, bulkheads dividing the sacred Internal Market, even in the face of a disaster like Covid-19, which may become the worst public health crisis since the Spanish Flu exactly a hundred years ago.

As always happens in Europe, when things got serious, the site of action moved to the national level. The European Central Bank had to admit that it had fired its last bullet some time ago when it lowered the euro interest rate to zero. So countries are left to their own devices fighting the approaching depression. The German government, in an unprecedented move, committed itself publicly to unlimited low-interest credit for firms getting into trouble; the argument for effectively giving up 'black zero' being that successful fiscal consolidation had enabled the German state to take up as much debt as it will take to support the German economy – 'and believe us, it will be enough'. Other countries, many already deeply in debt, will follow suit; what this will mean for the European political economy, the Eurozone and the financial sector will be sorted out later when the crisis will, perhaps, be over.

Right now European countries are struggling to get their health care systems ready for growing numbers of people requiring intensive care, over many months if not longer. In some countries national health care systems are already proving woefully inadequate, and here the EU comes back into the picture: with its unrelenting pressure on member states over decades to cut public spending and medical spending in particular, and open up health care for private investment and competitive markets – another case of neoliberal economizing on public budgets destroying redundant capacities above and beyond short-term needs.

Among the worst failures of the EU, which claims to represent 'the largest market in the world,' was that it did not learn the lesson of the two preceding epidemics, Sars1 seventeen years ago and Avian Flu a few years later. Apparently, according to a recent article in the *Frankfurter Allgemeine*, not a socialist newspaper by any means, developing vaccines against these sorts of diseases is not profitable enough for the uniquely profitable and highly globalized pharmaceutical industry. No effort seems to have been made by European governments, let alone the EU, to make the development, production and stockpiling of a vaccine against the next contagion, which insiders knew would inevitably come, a condition for market access in Europe. Moreover, essential components of the kind of medicines that are now needed are no longer being produced in Europe, as the pharmaceutical industry has relocated its production to China, of all places, where manufacturing came to a standstill because of the virus.

The neoliberal revolution made people forget that health care is an infrastructure that must be maintained as a public utility rather than a private money-making machine. Governments and international organizations neglect their basic duties if they fail to provide for the production at home, independent from fragile global production chains, of medications and other materials required for fighting epidemics like Covid-19. The parallels with the failure to re-regulate the global financial industry after 2008 to make it more responsive to the needs of real people in real countries are terrifyingly blatant; it is not just the Corona crisis that can repeat itself at any time but the financial crisis as well, and now perhaps together with and caused by the former.

15 April 2020
'European solidarity' – too little or too much?

Depends on what you mean by it. When it came to brutally forcing the Greek Syriza government to cut public spending, commit to a primary budget surplus and accept strict

conditionality for more loans instead of debt relief, the governments of Italy, Spain and France staunchly stood by Germany,
in a firm line of solidarity with Austria, Finland and the
Netherlands. Moreover, they worked hard to cut their own
spending, at the behest of Berlin and Brussels, in line with
Amsterdam rules, absurdly trying to achieve growth while
reducing debt through austerity to remain members in good
standing of that strange contraption, the Economic and
Monetary Union (EMU). As a result their economies stag-
nated while their public debt went up, in Italy from 119 per
cent of GDP in 2010 to 128 in 2019, in Spain from 62 to 95
per cent, in France from 81 to 96 per cent. In booming Germany,
on the other hand, public debt declined from 83 to 56 per
cent, below the Maastricht limit.

Does this matter? Spending on health care in 2017 was as low
as 8.8 per cent of GDP in Italy and 8.9 per cent in Spain. Of this
only 6.5 and 6.3 per cent, respectively, was publicly funded; the
rest was paid out-of-pocket or through voluntary health insurance schemes. German health care spending was 11.2 per cent in
2017, of which 9.5 per cent was public. The different impact of
Corona in different countries has complex causes, including
demographic structures, local air quality, ways of family life and
life in general, in particular of so-called 'risk groups' including
the aged, and the general health condition of the population –
but the endowment of national health care systems is certainly
one of them. Class structure matters, and so does access to
health care; the National Health Service of the United
Kingdom is allowed no more than 7.6 per cent of British GDP,
after decades of government-imposed austerity. In the United
States, with by far the highest health care spending in the world,
at 17.1 per cent of GDP, a huge part of the population is
without health insurance and cannot even afford a Corona test.

Looking at Europe and the EU, the relationship between
Corona deaths and the EMU austerity regime is obvious:

Germany prospers under the EMU, while Italy, Spain and France suffer – no money to make national health care systems fit for the risks that come with 'globalization', risks that have been well-known for a long time, not just since Sars1 in 2002 and 2003. Paying off your debt to qualify as a good debtor, welcome to take up new and more debt, trumps everything else, and perhaps the next virus will take its time and visit only after the political leaders of today have retired?

What has the EU done to correct this kind of 'European solidarity'? There are elaborate mechanisms to make countries stick to fiscal consolidation, including the so-called 'European semester' under the so-called 'Open Method of Coordination', rituals staged by that elusive Brussels technocracy whose ways only enthusiastic specialists perhaps understand. But what about coordination for the prevention of epidemics, or for health care generally? An extensive search reveals the existence of an EU agency called the European Centre for Disease Prevention and Control (ECDC), based in Stockholm, with 280 full-time staff and an annual budget of 57 million euros per year, of which no European citizen has ever heard, unless he or she happens to be an epidemiologist. Have they ever checked if member countries had enough facemasks, vaccines, ventilators, trained staff in case the next virus strikes? Have they, for example, held training courses for health care professionals and regulators on hospital hygiene, disease prevention in homes for the aged? Have they warned the European public that living the global life can be deadly unless you are prepared for it, and that getting prepared for it is anything but cheap? Of course, they have not – or at least nobody has heard of it, which amounts to the same thing, and it would be surprising if among the reasons for this wasn't the fact that such warnings would have conflicted with the budget consolidation warnings emitted year by year by the various austerity exercises that fueled the German export machine while depressing growth and raising debt in countries not made for a hard currency regime.

Today there is talk about a different kind of solidarity, which asks for the Northern states, the beneficiaries of the EMU, to bail out the Corona victims in the South, as a reward for their cooperation with austerity in general and the Greek 'rescue' in particular. Will they now, under the impetus of the Corona devastation, finally get what they have hitherto always demanded in vain, fiscal assistance without conditionality plus 'Eurobonds', now for a change called 'Coronabonds'? It seems beyond belief that the political classes of Southern Europe should not know that whatever they can extract from the North under the Maastricht regime will always fall under the Draghi-like verdict: Believe me, it won't be enough. Who could seriously expect the decade-long decay of Italy (and also of France) under the monetary and fiscal dictatorship of the EMU to be halted and indeed reversed by the injection of a few billion euros from Northern European taxpayers and the ECB? The most this can do is create a public relations opportunity for the 'pro-European', meaning pro-EMU, governments of the southern Eurozone to triumphantly report to their publics a historic victory over the stingy Dutch and Germans.

For a while, it may suffice to keep them in power, and for this Merkel and Co. are undoubtedly willing to pay significantly more than their national constitutions and the treaties allow. But keeping Salvini and Le Pen out is not the same as reviving the declining economies of those countries. Even bringing health care spending in Italy and Spain up to the German level, which would require more than two per cent of their GDP year by year, is completely out of reach for even the most generous 'transfer union'.

The real question, then, is why the political elites of countries condemned under the EMU to economic and social decline insist on remaining in the euro, rather than negotiating hard with their Northern European counterparts for a peaceful return, powered by a golden or even platinum handshake, to something like monetary and, with it, fiscal sovereignty – in other words: to politically accountable democracy? Could it be that they have already given up hope that they can effectively govern their countries under the capitalism of today, apart from symbolic cockfights with the Dutch and the Germans for the entertainment of their electorates? Are they still serious about democratic self-government, or are they trying to sneak under a Northern European imperial umbrella, where they will be governed as a Southern periphery by Brussels, meaning Berlin, with or without Paris?

We know the reasons why they wanted to join the EMU in the first place, and they are not necessarily pretty: to deploy a German-style common currency as a *vincolo esterno*, in the language of the Italian treasury, an external tie, as a tool for the 'modernization' of their unwieldy political economies through neoliberal 'structural reforms'. The Germans suspected that this might not really work and opposed the euro until Kohl concluded that he had to give in to Mitterand, for the sake of German reunification. Now, instead of 'structural reforms' producing economic happiness under the new European gold standard, we have austerity, economic decline, increasingly dysfunctional public infrastructure and what is called 'populist anti-Europeanism'.

How long will it take for the successors of the Southern 'modernizers' of the 1990s to realize that the problem with the EMU is structural, and therefore cannot be healed by moral rhetoric, and that the historic mistake of the Amsterdam Treaty must be undone rather than papered over with philanthropic 'solidarity' – not to mention the disconcerting possibility that capitalist modernization as such may have become a project of the past and that our societies may, as capitalist societies, become more and more ungovernable?

15 May 2020
State-building by stealth?

The Public Sector Purchase Programme (PSPP) ruling of the German Constitutional Court has laid bare yet another fault line in the edifice of the European Union, that between legal systems with different concepts of constitutional law.* There are parallels here to the UK, where the EU sort of constitution, written step by step by a court of last instance, clashed with a deeply rooted tradition of government by parliament, contributing to Brexit. In the conflict between the German Constitutional Court and the European Court of Justice we observe a fight between two powerful courts of last instance over which is the 'last of the last'. Also at stake is the nature of the EU as either an international organization or a federal state.

The strong position of the Constitutional Court in Germany is an essential part of the country's postwar political heritage. It is comparable to the provision in the German constitution that German troops cannot be deployed abroad, even under international command, without a narrowly defined parliamentary mandate. Both are limits on the discretion of the federal executive, and don't sit easily with another constitutional obligation on the German government to pursue international cooperation as a national priority.

The extensive powers of the Constitutional Court amount to an uncomfortable veto point for German government policy,

---

* The PSPP is a quantitative easing (QE) instrument of the European Central Bank (ECB) affiliates to buy marketable debt instruments of EU member states in order to create liquidity. While the ECB defends it as a tool of monetary policy – which is under its jurisdiction – the plaintiffs in the case before the GCC claimed it was in fact fiscal and economic policy, which the treaties assign exclusively to the member states. They also argued that the programme effectively amounted to monetary state funding, which is outlawed by the treaties.

both foreign and domestic. On the other hand, reference to the Court as a potential spoilsport can sometimes improve the country's international bargaining position. Moreover, the Court usually does its best to accommodate the government in power. In the PSPP case, for example, it didn't go so far as to bar the German central bank from participating in the ECB's bond purchasing programme. What it always insists upon, however, is its authority to decide whether actions by organs of the German state, here the Bundesbank, infringe on the democratic and political-constitutional rights of German citizens, on the grounds that such actions are not covered by German constitutional law or by international treaties lawfully ratified by the German state.

The implications of this case are far-reaching. Sticking to its constitutional guns, the Court insisted that the EU, ECB and ECJ cannot extend their jurisdiction to the constitutional rights of German citizens vis-à-vis the German state. While this may seem trivial, it points out that the European Union is not (yet) a federal state but depends on specific powers delegated to it by member states. As one of the judges said in a newspaper interview: 'As long as we are not living in a European state, the membership of a country is governed by that country's constitutional law.'

The ruling also insists that constitutions, including the de facto constitution of the EU, cannot be amended on the quiet. Nor can they be set aside in the midst of a crisis, following Carl Schmitt's infamous verdict, *Der Notstand ist die Stunde der Exekutive* (the hour of need is the hour of the executive) – not to mention the German saying, also found in English and Spanish, *Not kennt kein Gebot* (need knows no law). So, if you want the EU to be sovereign, the Court says, you are free to seek a formal revision of the treaties followed by referenda, where constitutionally required for treaty changes to become law. Federalism, why not, but in bright daylight please, not as a side-effect of ECB crisis management sanctioned by an activist European court. (Of course, a federalist revision of the treaties, in fact, any revision, is for all practical purposes out of the question, now and in any foreseeable future.)

It is interesting that the commentariat, right and left, fails to understand how embarrassed the German executive is about the Court's PSPP ruling, at a time when Germany is preparing to take over the presidency of the Union for the second half of 2020. Cooling down the rhetorical excitement over German tightfistedness may require the German state to pay more for its European hegemony than it can extract from its crisis-battered citizen-voters. Worse, the ruling has raised the question of all questions, one that European governments have learned painfully to avoid, namely what is the real *finalité* of the EU?

The temptation for the German political class to use the European outcry to get rid of the Constitutional Court must be enormous. This would expand the political leeway of the executive, in line with a general tendency in capitalist democracies – paralleling developments in Poland and Hungary, for example. Cutting the powers of the Court would not be easy, given its prestige among the German public. Still, a constitutional amendment turning it into a court of second-to-last instance behind the ECJ might go through, especially if the impression were somehow created that it would help against Corona and the economic disaster the virus may leave in its wake. The necessary two-thirds majority in the parliament could be found if the SPD and the Greens fill in for those CDU/CSU deputies refusing to vote in favour. Would this not be a nice present for Merkel to offer the European Council as Germany takes over the EU presidency on 1 July?

A downgrading of the German Constitutional Court should also be welcome to those who, like the philosopher Jürgen Habermas, call for a European army as a vehicle towards a European state. The need to get a mandate from the Bundestag is often a problem when Germany is asked to contribute troops to 'missions' in places like Iraq, Libya, Syria, Mali or Afghanistan. With the Constitutional Court out of the way, at least in international matters, the government would find it easier to override parliamentary opposition. Ursula von der Leyen, now President of the European Commission, will have been in situations in her previous capacity as German defence minister where she couldn't do the Americans or the French a favour because of predictable objections in the Bundestag. Now pursuing European military cooperation under French pressure, she would find a weakening of the Court helpful.

In any case, immediately after the Court announced its ruling, German Greens in the European Parliament called upon the Commission to start formal infringement proceedings against Germany, even though the German government had done nothing to implement the judgment, nor given any sign that it ever would. Von der Leyen, an old Merkel loyalist, immediately followed suit, expressing the fear that Eastern European countries like Poland might otherwise feel encouraged also to disobey the ECJ. In this context she parenthetically referred to the PSPP ruling as a violation of 'European sovereignty'. Infringement proceedings take time, and there will be quite a few member states wondering what it would do to their own sovereignty if the EU managed to claim sovereignty for itself; they may wait until the last minute to speak up, hoping that the Germans will slug it out for them. Most probably the proceedings will be halted or prevented from getting under way in exchange for Germany paying more into the next European budget, perhaps after having slaughtered its Constitutional Court as a sacrificial lamb on the altars of Europeanism.

Whatever else may happen, we can count on two things. Firstly, the German government will find ways to allow the ECB to carry on doing 'whatever it takes' to keep the euro alive. (Whether this will ultimately be successful is a different matter.)

The euro is the ultimate German bonanza, and while it is far from clear why Italy and Spain and France are so eager to hang on to it, for Germany, it is a lifeline in these times of secular capitalist stagnation.

Secondly, while the ECB, the Brussels budget, the European investment bank *e tutti quanti* may be able to find the means to keep the political classes of the Euroland's declining southern periphery in power for a few more years, through injections of European cash and skillfully staged German symbolic capitulations, such measures will do nothing to halt the economic devastation of the Mediterranean countries. The problem is structural, rooted in the abdication of monetary sovereignty, and so profound that it cannot be remedied by whatever transfers German governments can economically and politically cough up. Instead, we will see rising inequality, between countries and within them, and accelerating international hostility. The hour of truth is arriving for German empty promises, made in the reckless hope that they will never have to be redeemed, and the disappointment will be poisonous in the extreme.